When I finished reading the six plays in *Futures* I felt I'd become a vibrating point in an expanding, impending, defamiliarized world. The six playwrights included—Arzé Khodr, Wael Kadour, Leila Toubel, Sami Nasr, Rim Mejdi, Yasser Abu Shaqra—are each keenly distinct in their work and insight. Gathering them here in translation makes for a stunning, multifarious, explosive book. Displacements, hauntings, authoritarian shadows, linguistic power struggles, families severed and returned, choices and dark absences of choice, mercy and its opposites, remembering and forgetting among ghosts and migrations and others' dreams... These playwrights (and translators and editors) are preparing their audience, with love and imagination and lucid horror, for our own futures, grabbing our hands as the train picks up speed.

—Hilary Plum, author of *State Champ* and *Important Groups*

December 2025
Brooklyn, NY

Futures: An Anthology of Contemporary Arab Theater

53rdstatepress.org

ISBN Number: 979-8986581491

Book design: Kate Kremer
Cover image: Sky Lou Murray
Cover design: w/d

Printed on recycled paper in the United States of America.

Futures is made possible by the New York State Council on the Arts with the support of the Office of the Governor and the New York State Legislature.

An Anthology of Contemporary Arab Theater

FUTURES

Edited by Yasser Abu Shaqra + Agnes Borinsky

with plays by:
Yasser Abu Shaqra | Wael Kadour |
Arzé Khodr | Rim Mejdi | Sami Nasr |
Leila Toubel

translations by:
Hisham Ben Khamsa | Jonas Elbousty |
Caline Nasrallah | Clem Naylor

CONTENTS

WORDS THAT ENCAPSULATE OUR WORLD TODAY

In Leila Toubel's *Yakouta (Ruby)*, words flow in a harrowing monologue, addressing all the issues faced by abused, oppressed, and violated women in a society that projects its own malaise onto them and their bodies.

Similarly, in Sami Nasr's *Uprooting; or, The Dog and Cat Pizza Chapters*, words intensify; the language is shocking, unwavering, and unembellished, and does not falter or flinch as it decries cruelty, torture, terrorism, arms trafficking, food fraud, and electoral fraud.

In contrast, the use of everyday language in Arzé Khodr's *Sometimes we remember…* is excruciating as it gauges the scars of war, registering the way events settle into the subconscious. Words address simple, ordinary experiences. They record the traces left on characters who have fought, killed, and profited from war—and who have gone on to live with the resulting wound, cloaking it in a fragile veil of forgetfulness.

War memories are also the focus of Wael Kadour's *Braveheart*. Writing about writing becomes an attempt to purge the fear and the trauma of torture. The jailer merges with the lover, and the real becomes intertwined with the imaginary.

Migration, crossing seas, traversing forests, living in camps, and seeking family reunification are all explored in Yasser Abu Shaqra's *Left Out Gone Bad*, which depicts family members who have lived through estrangement, displacement, and loss. Uprooted from its natural context, the traditional family itself faces fragmentation.

As for *Eternity*, Rim Mejdi's play consolidates the multiple dimensions that subtly characterize our lives and distills them into a single mysterious incident. It sets existential questions about choosing to leave or die, stay or to go mad, against the backdrop of Rimbaud's poetry.

Despite the diversity of their themes and approaches to reality, these six new plays all address urgent contemporary issues with force and skill. They present a picture of modern life in a world that has reached the brink of the unthinkable.

With its painful and shocking treatment of reality, contemporary writing emerges here as it should: blunt and audacious, carving deep wounds into the soul as it depicts all this violence—to the point of unbearability.

These are texts that neither compromise nor seek to entertain; they do not bow to established norms and conventions. They scar because they are truthful, and their impact on the reader, whether through reading or performance, will transcend the old categories of fear and pity, going beyond mere identification or estrangement.

They emanate from us and they are for us. They map our own memory, describe our own reality, and express our own pain.

– Hanan Kassab Hassan

Sometimes

we

remember...

By Arzé Khodr

Translated by Clem Naylor and Arzé Khodr

To the memory of Elyse Dodgson.
Inspired by true stories.

ON *SOMETIMES WE REMEMBER...*

Sometimes we (can't help but) remember the temperature of the light that day, or the way their face lost dimension as the sun's totalitarian radiance shifted slightly to the left:

Sometimes we can't help but remember that prick of cold on our cheek from the open window:

Sometimes we can't help but remember the exact time on that old analog clock above the classroom door that could very well be 5 or 16 or 200 minutes off:

Sometimes we can't help but remember the smell of grass and sweet pepper wafting over our corneas, producing nostalgic barbeque tears:

Sometimes we can't help but remember the freckle on their right buttcheek, and how we traced a spiral around it with our tongue:

Sometimes we can't help but remember our hand stinging after we slapped the shit out of someone, on impulse, and how proud we felt to properly defend ourselves:

Sometimes we can't help but remember how they deserved much more than a slap, and how honorably we practiced restraint:

Sometimes we can't help but remember the things we have been told, over and over again like legend, and how they slowly hit our eardrums with grim certainty, turning our minds against their formerly pristine and curious nature, a patch garden overrun with dandelions and intrusivities, rattling in our skulls with fraught force, the loudest illusions:

Sometimes we forget, and then comes the shame, reckoning with a feeling-shaped hole, the knowledge of the lack of knowledge, this arid technology of desperation:

Sometimes we forget so hard that we squeeze ourselves dry of every sensation to which we've ever been subjected, shaken out on the floor of the shower with the piss and blood, just to prove that we can still be vessels of some fruitlessly objective truth:

Sometimes we can't help but remember how similar we are to those who seek to destroy us, and that this similarity is their manifesto:

Sometimes we choose not to remember how our breath and heartbeats sync up automatically, against our will, the terrifying ubiquity of oneness:

Sometimes we choose not to remember that memory is a choice.

— Nazareth Hassan

CHARACTERS

NADINE	33
AKRAM	34
SHOPKEEPER	early 40s
ROBERT	57
RAMZI	49

ACT I

SCENE ONE

2010. A bedroom in an apartment in Beirut. We see a man and a woman in their early thirties sleeping next to each other in a single bed. We hear a strange continuous noise coming from outside.

THE NOISE
Ta ta ta ta ta ta ta ta ta ......

NADINE *opens her eyes and starts moving, surprised. We hear the noise again.* NADINE *sits up in the bed. Her movement rouses* AKRAM, *who starts to wake up.*

NADINE
What's that?

AKRAM
That's Robert. (*He goes back to sleep.*)

NADINE
Who's Robert?

AKRAM
Robert, the one who shouts ... Go back to sleep ...

NADINE
What time is it?

She reaches out her hand to pick up her phone, which is on the bedside table, and looks at the time. She starts to get out of bed and pick up her clothes from the chair and floor.

AKRAM
You're leaving?

NADINE
I'm going home so I can get changed and go to work.

AKRAM
Wait a minute, I'll take you.

NADINE *starts getting dressed. We hear the shouting again.*

NADINE
What's wrong with that man so early in the morning?

AKRAM
(*Sitting up in bed*) Is this the first time you've heard him? He's always shouting. Went mad in the War.

NADINE
Seriously? Why?

AKRAM
Don't know. They say he was a sniper.

NADINE
(*Going to the window*) Where is he? (AKRAM *lies down again.*) Hey, Akram, where is he?

AKRAM
(*He opens his eyes again.*) He lives in the building down there.

NADINE
Do you know him?

AKRAM
(*He goes back to sleep.*) Ummm ...

NADINE
Can you hear me? Do you know him?

AKRAM
Yes my love, I've seen him around, he's an old man, he's harmless. Let me sleep a bit more.

NADINE
Okay, I'm going. I'll slam the door behind me. (*She's about to leave the room.*)

AKRAM
Where are you? Aren't you going to say goodbye?

NADINE *comes back, sits on the bed, and kisses him.*

NADINE
Do you want me to come back this evening?

AKRAM
As you like my love.

NADINE
You mean you won't miss me?

AKRAM
Of course I will my love.

NADINE
I'll miss you too. (*She kisses him.*)

AKRAM
(*He smiles in his sleep.*) I know.

He tries to go back to sleep. We hear the noise again: "Ta ta ta ta ta ta ta ta ta ta ta." NADINE *looks out of the window again, looking for* ROBERT.

SCENE TWO

The sitting room in AKRAM*'s apartment.* NADINE *is lying in front of the TV, with the remote control in her hand. Her shoes are in one corner of the room. In another corner, there is a table with bags of fast food on it.*

The doorbell rings continuously, NADINE *gets up and opens the door.* AKRAM *comes in, tired. He closes the door behind him. She hugs and kisses him.*

AKRAM
Phew, what's wrong with the lift? Didn't they turn on the generator today?

NADINE
There's power but the lift's broken.

AKRAM
Did you come up the stairs too?

NADINE
Only four floors. I got stuck in the lift, my love. It broke with me inside. Just my luck!

AKRAM
(*Joking*) Oh I see! So you wait until I give you the key to the place and then you come along and break everything…

NADINE
Yep, I only come to mess things up… (*She kisses him.*)

AKRAM
Who got you out of the lift then? Were you on your own?

NADINE
Yes I was on my own, don't you worry. And I wasn't scared because

I'm not claustrophobic like some people I know...

AKRAM
Go ahead, make fun of me. How long were you stuck there?

NADINE
Maybe ten minutes, quarter of an hour... To begin with, I just waited. I was thinking, "the generator'll come on now." But then, it was taking too long, so I started knocking on the door...

AKRAM
And the doorman heard you...

NADINE
And they called someone who did I don't know what, pulled the lift to the fourth floor, opened the door and got me out.

AKRAM
Did anyone ask where you were going?

NADINE
Oh, is that what you're worried about? (*Sharp*) The doorman knows where I'm going, he doesn't have to ask! What's the problem anyway? So what if they ask? So what if they know?

AKRAM
My love, you know people would talk... They'd start saying I'm bringing girls to the building, it wouldn't look good... I don't want anyone saying anything about you...

NADINE
So what if they did? They'd be talking about me, not you! It's no one else's business anyway.

AKRAM
I don't want anyone talking about my girlfriend!

NADINE
Phew! Seriously sometimes I feel like we're still living in the stone age. We're moving forward and you're still back there. We're at least

a hundred years ahead of you. Minimum! (*A short silence.*) Anyway, no one knows us here.

AKRAM

They know me now! And you don't know how rumours can spread. (*Trying to ease the tension*) My love, why do you always need to argue? (*He turns towards the bags on the table.*) You brought us dinner?

NADINE

Pizza.

AKRAM

Come on then, let's eat. Up you get...

NADINE

(*She gets up and gets a key out of her bag. She wants to put it on the table.*) Here's your key, Akram. I'd rather not have to deal with the responsibility.

AKRAM

(*He takes hold of her hand and closes it over the key.*) I made it for you. Keep it.

SCENE THREE

A small shop. There is a table with some groceries on it and several boxes with fruit and vegetables in them. The SHOPKEEPER *is a man in his early forties.* NADINE *is looking at a box of mangoes. She picks one up and smells it.*

NADINE
Where are these mangoes from?

SHOPKEEPER
Egypt, madam.

NADINE
Are they good?

SHOPKEEPER
Egyptian mangoes are the best, madam. Everyone knows that!

NADINE *picks some mangoes.*

NADINE
I'll take these.

The SHOPKEEPER *puts the mangoes on the scales and then into a bag.*

NADINE
And four bottles of beer, please.

SHOPKEEPER
Do you want them out of the fridge?

NADINE
Yes please. (*She picks a few things from the table.*) Oh, and I wanted to ask you about someone who lives here, somewhere next door, Robert.

SHOPKEEPER
Which Robert?

NADINE
The Robert who shouts.

SHOPKEEPER
Oh, that Robert. Why, what's wrong with him?

NADINE
Nothing. I was just wondering about him.

SHOPKEEPER
You want something from him? Are you from one of those institutions?

NADINE
Me? No! It's just that I've got friends who live here in the building behind, I heard him shouting, and I was told he went mad in the War. I was just curious.

SHOPKEEPER
Oh. Yes. It's like you were told. He went mad in the War.

NADINE
Which war?

SHOPKEEPER
Which war? The War!

NADINE
I got that. I meant the Two-Year War, the Mountain War, the Liberation War?[1] Which war?

SHOPKEEPER
Oh. What do I know... At the beginning of the War. He's been like this ever since I've known him.

NADINE
Was he in a militia?

1 Names given to specific periods of the Lebanese Civil War: the Two-Year War (1975-1976), the Mountain War (1983-1984), and the Liberation War (1989-1990).

SHOPKEEPER
Militia? So now they're militias? They were defending our land, our families!

NADINE
I didn't mean anything bad! I just said militia because that's what they call them now, after the War. (*She smiles apologetically.*) I really didn't mean anything bad. Sorry if I offended you.

The SHOPKEEPER *doesn't answer.*

SHOPKEEPER
Where are you from madam? Not round here?

NADINE
Why do you ask?

SHOPKEEPER
Because everyone here knows Robert!

NADINE
(*Smiling*) I am from here, from next door…

SHOPKEEPER
It's just that I've never seen you before…

NADINE
I just come to visit from time to time.

SHOPKEEPER
Right, so you're not from next door…

NADINE
You're asking me if I'm a Christian or a Muslim? I thought the War ended twenty years ago!

SHOPKEEPER
You come along and ask me about Robert, and you start talking about militias. What do you expect me to ask you?

NADINE

Alright, alright, I didn't mean to start all this trouble. Forget the whole thing. I was just making conversation. How much do I owe you?

SHOPKEEPER

Anyway, I'll tell you what they say. Robert was fighting...

NADINE

(*Interrupting*) Who for?

SHOPKEEPER

I don't know.

NADINE

You don't know?

SHOPKEEPER

It was at the beginning of the War. Who do you think he was fighting for?

NADINE

The Kataeb?[2]

SHOPKEEPER

Aren't you a clever one! He got injured in some fighting, they thought he was dead so they put him in the morgue with the rest of the dead bodies. He woke up with dead people all over him. Been mad ever since...

NADINE

Oh! Terrifying!

SHOPKEEPER

What do you think war's like? You didn't tell me where you're from exactly.

NADINE

From there. (*She smiles as she points towards the building that* AKRAM *lives in.*)

2 A Lebanese Christian party founded in 1936. It played a major role at the beginning of the Lebanese Civil War (1975-1990).

SCENE FOUR

The sitting room in AKRAM*'s apartment.* AKRAM *is working on the computer.* NADINE *comes out of the kitchen door.*

NADINE
Akram love, how many times do I have to tell you I can't wash up in cold water!

AKRAM
Well, what do you want me to do if there is no hot water in the kitchen?

NADINE
You could get someone to come and fix it!

AKRAM
Okay.

NADINE
That's the fifth time you've said okay.

AKRAM
I can't help it my love, I keep forgetting.

NADINE
Okay, you keep forgetting but I'm not going to keep freezing my hands. You do the washing up. (*She undoes the apron from around her waist.*)

AKRAM
You know I hate washing up.

NADINE
It's okay. Do it this time, and maybe next time you'll remember you've got to get someone to fix the water.

She sits down next to him.

AKRAM
(*Joking*) What's the point in having a woman if she thinks she's too good to do the dishes?

NADINE
Oh, I see! Just be upfront about it from the start, all you want is someone to do the dishes for you ...

AKRAM
(*Joking*) My love, bear in mind that when we get married, there'll be dishes to do every day.

NADINE
What if I don't want to?

AKRAM
I'm telling you now so that you will want to.

NADINE
If that's how it is, then I'll need to have a think about it ...

AKRAM
Really! You want to have a think about it! Then what? You'll change your mind? (*He moves towards her playfully.*)

NADINE
Stop it! Promise me you'll fix the water.

AKRAM
Darling, I told you I keep forgetting. Why don't you see if you know someone ...

NADINE
Ask the doorman, he'll definitely know someone.

AKRAM
Okay, fine. I'll ask the doorman.

NADINE
You won't forget?

AKRAM
No, I won't forget.

NADINE
(*She looks towards the computer.*) What are you doing?

AKRAM
I've got some work I want to finish by tomorrow.

NADINE
As usual. Pfff. Doesn't bank work finish at the bank?

AKRAM
I'm doing some research.

NADINE
Do you have to do it today?

AKRAM
My God, you do love to moan! Yes, I have to! I'm preparing for a workshop.

NADINE
What workshop?

AKRAM
A workshop we're doing for the staff.

NADINE
Oh. It's extra work?

AKRAM
Yes, and it's in Syria.

NADINE
When?

AKRAM
Next month.

NADINE
When next month?

AKRAM
The 9th.

NADINE
Will you stay there long?

AKRAM
Just three weekends, a couple of days each trip. Let me finish, love...

NADINE
But I'm bored! Let's go to the cinema...

AKRAM
Tomorrow, love. I can't now.

NADINE
You never can. We don't do anything! We just sit around at home.

AKRAM
What do you mean "sit around at home"? Didn't we go out with your work friends on Saturday?

NADINE
Not last Saturday, the one before. (*Short silence.* AKRAM *continues to work.*) Since I started coming to your place, we've stopped going out at all.

AKRAM
Love, why are you being like this? Why do you think I work this much?

NADINE
For the money.

AKRAM
Okay, for the money. And what's money for?

NADINE
...

AKRAM

Answer me! What's money for? So we can buy an apartment and get married, isn't it?

NADINE

Yes.

AKRAM

Well, then, if you know that, what's bothering you? You're always moaning, you're always unhappy!

NADINE

You're right. I am unhappy!

AKRAM

Why are you unhappy?

NADINE

I don't know.

AKRAM

Who does?

NADINE

Stop it!

AKRAM

No! Tell me what's bothering you. You're healthy, you've got a job, you're going to get married, what more do you want?

NADINE

...

AKRAM

Tell me what's bothering you? Me? Us? You want us to break up?

NADINE

No. (*Silence.*) I want to go to the cinema.

She gets up, picks her bag up from the table and goes out.

SCENE FIVE

The little shop.

NADINE
Hello.

SHOPKEEPER
Hello, madam. How are you today?

NADINE
Fine, all good. I've got some questions for you today too.

SHOPKEEPER
About Robert? I told you everything I know.

NADINE
No, I want to ask you about someone else. The man who fixes lifts and does odd jobs. I was told he lives near the shop.

SHOPKEEPER
You mean Ramzi?

NADINE
Yes, that's the one. They gave me his number but he's not picking up. They told me he lives near here.

SHOPKEEPER
He lives in that building there. (*He points to the left.*) Go up the stairs, there's a room on the rooftop. That's where he is.

NADINE
Thanks.

SHOPKEEPER
What is it, is the lift broken or do you want to ask him about Robert?

NADINE
Robert?

SHOPKEEPER
The Robert who shouts, have you already forgotten?

NADINE
Oh, no. I want him to fix the hot water for the sink. Why, what's it got to do with Robert?

SHOPKEEPER
Ramzi's Robert's brother.

NADINE
Really? His brother? (*She points to the left.*) So that's where they live?

SHOPKEEPER
Yes.

NADINE
Alone?

SHOPKEEPER
Robert's always alone, and when Ramzi's here he stays with him.

NADINE
So he's not always here?

SHOPKEEPER
Ramzi's always travelling.

NADINE
And is he here now or not? I just need him to fix the hot water.

SHOPKEEPER
He's here now.

NADINE
Could he be going away again soon? Where does he go?

SHOPKEEPER
Madam, you seem to be very curious. Go up there and ask yourself.

NADINE
Fine. Thanks.

SHOPKEEPER
Don't you want any mangoes today?

NADINE
If there are any. I'll get them on the way back.

SHOPKEEPER
Alright then. See you later.

SCENE SIX

NADINE *arrives on the roof. In the middle of it, there is a room with its door ajar. She knocks on the door. We hear the voice of a man inside.*

THE VOICE
Come in.

NADINE *pushes the door and goes in. We see* ROBERT, *a man in his fifties. He looks old and very thin. He is wearing an old tracksuit, his hair is white and he has a thin beard. He is sitting on an old, narrow bed in front of a small TV. There is a table in front of him with some leftover food on it. There are bits of clothing scattered over the floor.*

This room leads onto another room, in which we see a sofa with a lot of clothes on it, and a large TV, which is on. There are two packs of cigarettes in front of ROBERT. *He holds them in his hand and passes them from one hand to the other. He rubs his arm and then he lights a cigarette. He smokes half of it and then throws it onto the floor. The floor is covered with butts of half smoked cigarettes.*

NADINE *contemplates the room and the man.*

NADINE
Are you Robert?

ROBERT
Yes.

NADINE
How are you?

ROBERT
Fine, how are you two? Well, I hope?

NADINE
Well, thanks. (*Silence.*) Can I sit down?

ROBERT *pats the bed to indicate that she should sit next to him.* NADINE *sits down and contemplates the scene.* ROBERT *smokes, and when he stops, he starts tracing his finger along the circular shapes on the bedspread. From time to time, he also looks at the TV. He seems to be in another world.* NADINE *observes him.*

ROBERT
(*Pointing at the screen, when the billionaire Carlos Slim appears*) That man emigrated to Brazil.

NADINE
Mexico.

ROBERT
Mexico, Brazil, they all speak Portuguese.

NADINE
You've heard about him too?

ROBERT
He went away and he came back. Maybe he came to get married. Lots of people who emigrate come back to get married.

ROBERT *mumbles and only half of what he says is comprehensible, though we can work out what he is talking about.*

NADINE
He has a lot of money! He's the richest man in the whole world.

ROBERT
He's afraid someone might do something to him.

Silence. NADINE *is stunned by* ROBERT*'s character and is searching for something to talk about.*

NADINE
Were you married? Did you have kids?

ROBERT
Yes ... (*He mumbles something incomprehensible.*)

NADINE *observes* ROBERT, *the room, and its contents in amazement. She tries to think of topics that will make* ROBERT *talk.*

NADINE
Do you work?

ROBERT
Now, no. At home.

NADINE
You used to work before?

ROBERT
Yes, for the government.

NADINE
What did you do for the government?

ROBERT *doesn't answer. When he doesn't say anything, he looks into the distance and mutters. From time to time, a very worried expression comes over his face, he seems to be on the point of saying something and then he doesn't.*

NADINE
What work did you do for the government?

ROBERT *doesn't answer. They watch TV, which is showing a scene of a man and a woman lying in bed together.*

ROBERT
Everything goes through the censors.

NADINE
Do you watch a lot of TV?

ROBERT *mumbles something incomprehensible. A famous Lebanese singer comes on the TV,* ROBERT *recognizes him.*

ROBERT
Melhem Barakat.

NADINE
Wow. You know singers! Do you know politicians too?

ROBERT
Yes, yes.

NADINE
Like who?

ROBERT *mumbles.*

NADINE
Do you know Hariri?[3]

ROBERT
Yes.

Silence. NADINE *looks towards the other room, where the TV is on, but it's on mute.*

NADINE
Why did you put the TV on in there?

ROBERT
Ramzi's sleeping.

---

3 Saad Hariri was the Prime Minister of Lebanon from 2009 to 2011 and 2016 to 2019. He is the son of the former Prime Minister Rafic Hariri, who was assassinated in 2005 in downtown Beirut.

NADINE
Is that your brother?

ROBERT
Yes, my brother. When he was born, he weighed eleven pounds. They gave her a caesarean and she died.

NADINE
Who? Your mum?

ROBERT
Yes.

NADINE
Really? When you were small? Do you remember it?

ROBERT
Ramzi was born in 1960, the girl in 1950, Joseph in 1953. (*He starts counting on his fingers and loses track of the numbers.*)

ROBERT
52, 53, 68…

NADINE
Do you remember anything from the War?

ROBERT
I was at the Catholic school.

NADINE
Where?

ROBERT
Bourj Hammoud.

NADINE
What was it called? Do you remember? (*Silence.*) What else do you remember?

ROBERT *seems lost and unable to answer* NADINE*'s questions. He mutters some incomprehensible* *words.* NADINE *looks in her pocket for her phone so that she can check the time.*

ROBERT
If you've lost your wallet, go to the Red Cross. They know everything. They can tell you where you live.

NADINE
What?

ROBERT
At the Red Cross, they take blood for operations.

NADINE
Yes.

ROBERT
Are you from the Red Cross?

NADINE
No. I have friends living in the building behind here.

ROBERT
Everyone left, they went away...

NADINE
Where to?

ROBERT
Their villages.

NADINE
And where's your village?

ROBERT *says something incomprehensible.*

NADINE
What?

ROBERT
Zahlé.

NADINE
That's far!

ROBERT
Yes, but everyone has a car these days.

NADINE
But there's traffic.

ROBERT
Not much now.

NADINE
True. Rush hour's in the evening.

In the next room, where the TV is on, there is a bed against the wall. The cover moves. RAMZI *wakes up.* NADINE *stands up.*

NADINE
Hello.

RAMZI *is now sitting on the bed, he looks towards the room which* NADINE *is in. He's in his late forties, gaunt and hard-featured.*

RAMZI
Hi.

NADINE
Sorry to disturb you.

RAMZI
No, not at all. Sorry the flat's in such a state. How can I help you?

RAMZI *stands up and comes into the room where* NADINE *and* ROBERT *are. He stays standing as if in a rush.*

NADINE
I don't know if you remember me, that time you came to fix the lift

in the building behind … (*She points in the opposite direction.*) I was stuck in it …

RAMZI
Yes, now I remember you. Did the lift stop working again?

NADINE
No. I've got a problem with the hot water … It's not coming into the kitchen sink …

RAMZI
But madam, I'm a lift maintenance man.

NADINE
I know! But the doorman told me you do all sorts of odd jobs. I got your number from him, but you didn't pick up.

RAMZI
I don't answer calls from numbers I don't know.

NADINE
Oh. (*Short silence.*) Is there any chance you could come and have a look at the sink?

RAMZI
I can come but I can't promise I'll be able to do anything …

NADINE
…

RAMZI
Don't worry. If I can't help, I'll tell you where to find a plumber.

NADINE
Thank you. You're too kind. Do you want to come with me now?

RAMZI
I can't now. Tell me what floor you live on and maybe I'll come by on Monday afternoon.

SCENE SEVEN

Evening in AKRAM*'s sitting room.* AKRAM *is sitting, working in his usual place, behind the computer.* NADINE *enters from the bedroom. It looks like she has just put on her clothes.*

AKRAM
Hey, you got dressed?

NADINE
I want to sleep at home. I'm going up to the village tomorrow.

AKRAM
Don't you have to work?

NADINE
I've got a day off. I'll be back on Monday. Maybe Sunday evening...

AKRAM
(*While he continues working on the computer*) What's going on back in the village?

NADINE
My nephew's birthday. And the weather's nice. Do you want to come up on Saturday? My mum keeps on asking after you.

AKRAM
Really? And what do you say to her?

NADINE
I say you're well...

AKRAM
(*While focusing on the computer screen*) And...

NADINE
That you're very busy...

AKRAM
And …

NADINE
That you're always on the computer, that you make me do the washing up in cold water, that I like to sleep at your place even though your bed is small …

AKRAM
Seriously?

NADINE
What?

AKRAM
You tell her you sleep at my place?

NADINE
But I'm always at your place!

AKRAM
Are you crazy? What if your dad found out?

NADINE
So what?! What would he do?

AKRAM
He'd kill me!

NADINE
Are you serious? (*Making fun of him a little*) You? Why would he kill you? It's me he'd kill! Or maybe he'd kill us both … When you're the killing type, you might as well … I'm joking … Of course I don't tell my mother I sleep with you. But can it really never have crossed her mind? I'm thirty-three now, does she seriously think I'm going to wait till I get married? Why are you so scared anyway?

AKRAM
I'm not scared!

NADINE

What's the worst that could happen? We get married now rather than in a couple of years.

AKRAM

My love, you know I can't now ... Let's wait till we've saved a bit so we can put down a deposit on a flat and have a wedding ... Be patient!

NADINE

(*She approaches him reassuringly.*) Okay my love, I'm patient, I'm very patient. Get up and take me home. (*Her mobile rings. She moves away from Akram to answer it. She looks at the screen.*) It's my mum. (*On the phone*) Hi mum ... Fine. You? ... Yes, everything is good ... At home ... Yes, I'm coming tomorrow ... Okay. I'll pick them up on the way ... Today? Let me think ... Green beans ... Yes, delicious. I did them like you taught me. Course they weren't as good as yours though ... Yes ... Really? Where did she get it done? ... Great! And it looks nice? ... Yes, the swelling'll go down ... No, I don't want to. It's my nose and it's no one else's business ... I'm not annoyed but you've told me twice now ... Yes ... Okay ... Yes I'm seeing him ... Yes I told him, but he can't make it ... I will. Stop wasting your money on the phone.[4] We'll talk tomorrow. Bye mum.

AKRAM

What's up with my mother-in-law?

NADINE

She said my cousin Lara has had a nose job and it looks really nice, so why don't I get one too?

AKRAM

(*Smiling*) Tell her Akram loves me just the way I am ... There's a girl at the bank who's had a boob job, now that might be worth thinking about ...

NADINE

Oh really???

4 In 2010, Lebanon had some of the world's highest mobile phone service prices.

AKRAM
I'm joking, I'm joking!

NADINE
And she says hi.

AKRAM
Maybe we could go and visit your parents next Friday.

NADINE
Okay, if you like ... I met Robert today.

AKRAM
Who?

NADINE
Robert, the one who shouts.

AKRAM
(*Continues to focus on the computer*) Really? What, on the street?

NADINE
No, I went up to where he lives. He's so out of it. Really very strange. Have you ever spoken to him?

AKRAM
No.

NADINE
His brother was there too. His brother ... He's so tough ... There's something scary about him ... He's going to come and fix the water for us. I don't know how he can live with Robert. The flat's all messy and dirty, the floor's covered with cigarettes ... Are you listening to me?

AKRAM
Yes ...

NADINE
Are you still working on the workshop? (*She goes towards the computer screen.*) You're playing a game??? I knew it! (*She tries to stop him playing.*)

AKRAM
Wait a minute Nadine, please!!!

NADINE
Get up, come on get up. I want to go home now. Are you going to make me go home on my own in the dark?

AKRAM
Just a second…

NADINE
If you don't get up now, I'll go on strike. I won't set foot in your place for the whole of next week!

AKRAM
You can't do that!

NADINE
Why not? (AKRAM *doesn't reply, he's absorbed in his game.*) Yeah, why can't I?

AKRAM
Aaaargh… I lost. Happy now? You can't because you'll miss me.

NADINE
(*She comes near him.*) Oh, whereas you don't care at all?

AKRAM
What do you think?

NADINE
I don't know!

AKRAM
You don't know?

NADINE
No. Maybe we should try it, to see if you'll really miss me…

SCENE EIGHT

AKRAM's flat. The sitting room. RAMZI is sitting down and NADINE is giving him coffee.

RAMZI

Thanks. You're too kind…

NADINE

It's no trouble. You're welcome. So, what's the solution?

RAMZI

It's like I said, you need to install a separate boiler for the sink, in the ceiling space in the kitchen.

NADINE

And can you do it?

RAMZI

I can install it, but you need to buy one first.

NADINE

Me? Where from?

RAMZI

They sell them at lots of places. Your husband'll know where.

NADINE

(*A little embarrassed*) I don't think he knows about that sort of thing…

RAMZI

Do you want me to find out for you and let you know?

NADINE

I'd really appreciate that.

They drink their coffee in silence.

NADINE

There's something I'd like to ask you about.

RAMZI

(*Cautiously*) Yes?

NADINE

You're Robert's brother...

RAMZI

Yes. What's the problem? Is the shouting bothering you? You'll get used to it.

NADINE

No, I didn't mean that...

RAMZI

Anyway, he's totally harmless. He just shouts from time to time. Everyone's used to him by now.

NADINE

No, honestly I didn't mean that, I just wanted to ask how he... got to be like that... (*She seems embarrassed and unable to express herself.*)

RAMZI

How he went mad? He went mad in the War, didn't they tell you?

NADINE

Was there something particular that happened?

RAMZI

What happened happened and now he's how he is. Why do you care?

NADINE

I'm just curious, that's all!

RAMZI

What do you do madam? Are you a journalist?

NADINE

No.

RAMZI

Because if you're a journalist or a photographer or whatever, we won't have stories about our family or Robert's problems being sold for other people's entertainment!

NADINE
I promise you I'm not a journalist and I don't want to sell anyone's stories! I work in a bank ... It's just strange for someone like him to be living on his own like that ...

RAMZI
Who said he's on his own? We all take care of him, my sisters and me. My sister sends him food everyday with the cleaner. She washes his clothes, buys him cigarettes. And me, most of the time, if I'm not away, I live with him.

NADINE
I mean ... maybe someone like him should be in a home, or a hospital ...

RAMZI
Why? What's wrong with him? He's living in peace, no one's ever complained about him. Everyone in the neighborhood loves him. What does he do? He walks about on the street and shouts! It's no one else's business!

RAMZI *stands up.*

NADINE
You haven't finished your coffee ...

RAMZI
Thank you.

NADINE
Sorry if I asked too many questions.

RAMZI
It's okay. You're new here, can't blame you. There are people who knew him before he was like this. He was very popular back then. (*He heads for the door.*) I'll ask around about the boiler and let you know.

SCENE NINE

AKRAM's living room. AKRAM is working on the computer. The doorbell rings. AKRAM opens the door. It's RAMZI.

RAMZI
Morning. Is the lady in?

AKRAM
Which lady?

RAMZI
(*He looks at the bell, where there should be a name written.*) Isn't this the 8th floor? Yes, this is definitely the place!

AKRAM
Oh, you mean Nadine!

RAMZI
I asked about the boiler for her …

AKRAM
Let me just call her to see if she's coming today. If she is, she'll be on her way now.

AKRAM picks up his mobile and calls NADINE.

AKRAM
Nadine, hi, are you coming today? … There's a man here … (*He turns towards RAMZI, asking his name.*)

RAMZI
Ramzi.

AKRAM
Ramzi. He's come about the boiler … Okay. Okay. Bye. (*To RAMZI*) She can't make it today.

RAMZI
Are you her husband?

AKRAM
Almost …

RAMZI
But this is your place?

AKRAM
Yes.

RAMZI
Should I tell you about the different boilers and prices I found?

AKRAM
No, no. Nadine'll be here tomorrow. You can explain it all to her. This whole thing about the hot water for the sink was her idea anyway. If you can come round tomorrow afternoon, she'll definitely be here.

SCENE TEN

NADINE *is in* ROBERT*'s flat on the roof. She is sitting on a chair facing the bed. The room is still covered with cigarette butts and hasn't been tidied.* ROBERT *is smoking and watching TV, as usual.*

NADINE
How are you?

ROBERT
Fine thanks. You're most welcome.

NADINE
Has Ramzi been gone for long?

ROBERT
A long, long time.

NADINE
Do you know where he went?

ROBERT
He went out with his friends.

NADINE
Oh, okay. (*She looks at* ROBERT *with amazement.*) Do you ever go with him?

ROBERT
Sometimes they go, they go to watch the war.

NADINE
Which war?

ROBERT
The Iraq War.

NADINE
Really? The Iraq War?

ROBERT
Iraq, over there, far away.

NADINE
If it's far away, where do they watch it from?

ROBERT
From the balcony. You see everything from there.

NADINE
True. I used to watch the shells falling from the balcony too. You could see them clearly. Where they were being fired and where they were falling. You don't forget that, do you?

ROBERT *mumbles something.*

NADINE
Did you use to watch the War as well?

ROBERT
The street.

NADINE
Sorry?

ROBERT
I watch the street.

NADINE
What do you watch on the street?

ROBERT
The motorway, cars ... People go shopping. Every day.

NADINE
Yeah, you're right there. That's all they do.

NADINE *picks up her bag. She opens it, takes out a small packet of biscuits, opens it and gives a biscuit to* ROBERT. *He takes it and eats it.*

NADINE
Do you like it?

ROBERT
I like olives.

NADINE
Olives are the best. (ROBERT *finishes his biscuit so she gives him another. He takes it and eats it.*) Did you have lunch today?

ROBERT
I ate, I ate.

NADINE
What did you eat?

The usual worried look comes over ROBERT'*s face, as if he's thinking about something. He starts to mumble.* NADINE *sighs. She has given up trying to have a reasonable conversation with* ROBERT.

NADINE
I'm going now. Will you tell Ramzi I came?

ROBERT
Ramzi's going to be very late. He's out with the lads. A get-together. If he's having a good time he'll stay out, if not he'll come back.

NADINE
Should I write him a note?

ROBERT
He can't read or write. He doesn't know how.

NADINE
Really?

ROBERT
He went to watch the Iraq War.

NADINE
I got that. (*She grabs her bag and stands up to leave.*)

ROBERT
Stay. He'll be back at four. After sunset.

RAMZI *comes in.*

RAMZI
Stay. It's not sunset yet.

NADINE
I was waiting for you … How are you? Hope you're well …

RAMZI
All good. Thanks.

NADINE
You didn't come back for the boiler. I waited for you the next day.

RAMZI
(*Coldly*) I didn't have time. You could have called.

NADINE
But last time you told me you don't answer calls from numbers you don't know. And I didn't give you mine …

RAMZI
I asked about the prices and wrote them down for you. I'll go and get the list from inside. And give Robert a break, he won't know how to answer your questions.

NADINE
We were just talking …

RAMZI
I heard … And I heard last time too. (ROBERT *is watching the TV, not paying attention to the conversation.* NADINE *is still standing ready to leave,* RAMZI *comes close to her and asks quietly.*) What are you trying to do? Check if he's really crazy?

NADINE
No, not at all!

RAMZI
(*Showing her the way out of the apartment to the rooftop*) Is it like a show for you? Bit of entertainment? He makes you laugh?

NADINE
No, of course not! I'm trying to see if he remembers anything…

RAMZI
Why?

NADINE
Just because. I'd like to know… I like stories from the War! Pictures, books, archives! Robert is those old pictures, he is those war films… They told me he woke up in the morgue, surrounded by corpses, and that that moment he lost his mind. And there were others who said he was a sniper…

RAMZI
You've really done your research, haven't you?

NADINE
Is it true what they said?

RAMZI
No. It's not. And don't talk about the War to him because he gets upset, and starts the shouting business. (*Short silence.*) Oh, and you didn't tell me you weren't married.

NADINE
You didn't ask. (*Short silence.*) Does it make any difference to the boiler?

RAMZI
No, it doesn't. Wait here, I'll go and get the list.

SCENE ELEVEN

AKRAM's kitchen. There is a ladder going up to the ceiling space. NADINE is standing next to the ladder, looking towards the top, where RAMZI is fitting a boiler.

NADINE
Is it okay?

We hear the sound of tools.

RAMZI
It will be. (*The sound of tools continues, then RAMZI looks down from the ceiling space.*) Now it's okay. (*He makes his way down the ladder.*) I need to wash my hands please ...

NADINE
Sure, go ahead.

She points to the sink, then puts water on the hob to make coffee.

RAMZI
Don't trouble yourself, no need for coffee this time.

NADINE
It's no trouble at all! You've been slaving away for the past two hours! Take a seat, please.

RAMZI
(*Sitting on a chair near the kitchen table*) Thanks. Switch the boiler on to see if it works.

NADINE switches the boiler on, then starts making coffee.

RAMZI
There shouldn't be any problems, but if there are just let me know.

NADINE
Okay. Thanks.

RAMZI
You've got a broken drawer ...

NADINE
I know, and a shelf that's fallen off in the sitting room, and a broken wardrobe door in the bedroom ... There are a lot of things that need fixing in this place.

RAMZI
I can fix them if you want ...

NADINE
Not today. Akram'll be back soon, I still need to make him something.

RAMZI
Okay, I won't keep you then.

NADINE
No, no, stay. The coffee's ready.

RAMZI
Sorry to ask but ... Are you two engaged?

NADINE
Officially, with a ring?

RAMZI
Yes.

NADINE
No.

RAMZI
Oh. I asked around about you, and I found out you're not from around here, I mean Mr. Akram isn't.

NADINE
True. Akram's from Sawfar, and I'm from a small village in the

Shouf. (*She offers him coffee.*)

RAMZI

So you're from our Druze brothers ... You're most welcome. It's more convenient for you, isn't it? To live here with us ...

NADINE

It's closer to work.

RAMZI

Where do you work?

NADINE

In Hamra. (*Correcting herself*) I live in Hamra, I'm not always here.

RAMZI

I got that.

NADINE

But Akram works nearby.

RAMZI

And when you get married, you're also planning to live here?

NADINE

We haven't decided yet. But I don't think so ...

RAMZI

(*Sarcastic*) If you're comfortable in our neighborhood, why not? Now the country isn't like it used to be, now we're all brothers ... Better you than strangers.

NADINE

Flats here are so expensive now. I don't know ...

RAMZI

Looks like he's not in a hurry ... Listen, I'm going to tell you something, but don't take it the wrong way, you seem like a nice girl ... If he really loved you, he'd marry you, no one leaves a girl in their house without marrying her.

NADINE
That's your opinion. I don't have to justify myself to you. Are you married?

RAMZI
No. Wasn't lucky enough.

NADINE
Oh, yes. (*She smiles.*) It's always about luck…

RAMZI
Honestly? I haven't had the time!

NADINE
Lift maintenance keeps you that busy?

RAMZI
Not just lift maintenance.

NADINE
Oh! You've got another job too?

RAMZI
Before I was in the War. The whole way through. And on the side I learned how to fix lifts…

NADINE
Were you with Robert in the War?

RAMZI
Robert's older than me. He only fought for two years, before me. I'm still fighting.

NADINE
What do you mean? The War ended twenty years ago!

RAMZI
War never ends. I came back from Iraq two months ago.

NADINE
What's in Iraq?

RAMZI
War. And I'm a fighter. That's my main job.

NADINE
Who are you fighting for in Iraq?

RAMZI
For the Americans! Don't you follow the news?

NADINE
Not always ...

RAMZI
There were lots of stories about us in the papers.

NADINE
Who's "us"?

RAMZI
The Lebanese who fight for the Americans.

NADINE
Oh.

RAMZI
Yes. The Americans need us: we speak Arabic, we've got battle experience, and we're Christian. They trust us. Although, believe me, we're not like them at all ...

NADINE
So you work with the American army?

RAMZI
I work with an American security company. We do security for the VIPs there.

NADINE
And before, during the War here in Lebanon, were you in the Lebanese Forces?[5]

5 Al Quwat al Lubnaniya (The Lebanese Forces) were a Christian Lebanese militia

RAMZI
Yes.

NADINE
Were you in the Mountain War?

RAMZI
Yes I was.

NADINE
Me too.

RAMZI
Why, how old were you?

NADINE
Seven.

RAMZI
What could you possibly remember?! What would you know about what happened? It wasn't you who got driven out, it wasn't you who got slaughtered!

NADINE
(*She wants to react to his last sentence. But she restrains herself. Short silence.*) My dad and my brother fought in the Mountain War…There was a basement under our house. They caught a fighter from the Lebanese Forces and locked him up down there.

RAMZI
(*Sarcastic*) And you used to visit him and give him food?

NADINE
No. He used to scream a lot because my dad and brother were torturing him. "Oh mother, Oh Mary." Screams. It was deafening. My mother was going mad. My sister was sixteen. One night, after they finished torturing him, after he had stopped shouting, she got up quietly, I saw her and ran after her. She told me to go back to bed, but I refused.

---

who played a major role in the Civil War. After the War, they became a political party.

I went down to the basement with her and we saw him. The bones in his lower arms were showing. I don't know how they were taking off his skin, like flaying him slowly, they even started to scrape his bones ... His arms ... I remember them perfectly ... That was why he was shouting. My sister untied him and helped him escape ... When my dad found out, he went crazy. He locked her in the basement for a whole month, and didn't speak to her for three years. If it weren't for my mum, he probably would've taken the skin off her arms too.

RAMZI

Lucky guy that they decided to play with him! Didn't slit his throat right away and throw him in the well! How many bodies still haven't been found? Whole families ...

NADINE

Do you know anyone who survived the Mountain War and had no skin on their arms?

RAMZI

No.

NADINE

I remember my sister dragged him up to the main road, because he couldn't walk. We didn't hear anything about him after that. Do you think he made it?

RAMZI

I don't know ... That's why you like war stories? You're still looking for him?

NADINE

Every time I hear someone was with the Lebanese Forces, I try to ask questions, but no one wants to talk. The whole war, no one wants to talk about it, never mind the Mountain War. Especially now after the reconciliation[6] ...

---

6 "The Reconciliation Agreement" (Musalaha) was the name given to the symbolic agreement between the Christians and the Druze after the War. It aimed to build trust between the two sides after the Mountain War (1983), which witnessed horrific massacres and caused the displacement of Christian civilians.

RAMZI

What do you want with those stories anyway? They're useless. Focus on your work and on your life, and try out the boiler. And if you want to fix the drawer or the shelf or anything else, let me know. I'm here for now.

SCENE TWELVE

AKRAM's kitchen. NADINE is preparing food. She takes vegetables out of the fridge to wash them, then she starts peeling some potatoes, humming as she does so. AKRAM comes in quietly. He is carrying a small suitcase. It looks like he has come back from a trip. Suddenly he drops the suitcase on the floor, it makes a loud noise and NADINE shrieks in fear. AKRAM laughs.

NADINE

How many times have I told you I hate it when people frighten me like that! There's nothing to laugh about!

AKRAM

I can't not laugh! I keep doing it and you keep losing it!

NADINE

(*Mocking him by using his tone of voice*) You think you're funny?

AKRAM

That's how you welcome me, is it? I've been out of the country for two whole days!

NADINE

It's not like you crossed the ocean! Damascus is practically round the corner ... You're back early this time.

AKRAM

We finished a bit early and there wasn't much traffic at the border. What are you cooking?

NADINE

Kafta[7] and potatoes. I brought the kafta from the village. And salad. But I haven't started yet. If you're really hungry, start washing the

7 A traditional Middle Eastern dish made with ground meat, chopped parsley, minced onions, and spices.

vegetables. And if you don't feel like it, just wait a little, it won't take long.

He leaves the kitchen.

NADINE
When will you take me with you to Damascus?

AKRAM
We've got time for that. (*He comes into the kitchen carrying a box of sweets. He puts it on the table.*) I brought you Ghraybeh.[8]

NADINE
(*Sarcastic*) For me? Thanks. I will kill you if I catch you eating them in bed. You keep covering the sheets with crumbs!

AKRAM *opens the box and starts eating.*

NADINE
How many more trips have you got till you finish the workshop? One more, no?

AKRAM
Yes. Next week.

NADINE
Book your hotel room for an extra night, I'll join you on Saturday, and we'll spend Sunday there.

AKRAM
I already said we've got time ...

NADINE
Do we? When?

AKRAM
I might ask to move to the Damascus branch.

---

8 A type of biscuit made with ghee that is famous in the Middle East and especially in Syria.

NADINE
Why?

AKRAM
I'd get a huge pay rise!

NADINE
But you'd have to move there, wouldn't you?

AKRAM
Love, you just said Damascus was practically round the corner! And we have to make sacrifices so we can get married…

NADINE
…

AKRAM
Don't worry my darling. I'd come here every Friday and Saturday, and you could come to Damascus whenever you wanted. There's no need to worry. A year, two maximum, they'd fly by! Lots of people at the bank work in Damascus, some of them are married and have children! They come back on weekends, it's no big deal!

NADINE
So that's it, you've made up your mind and you're just letting me know?

AKRAM
I'm not 100% sure yet.

NADINE
(*Sarcastic*) 80%?

SCENE THIRTEEN

AKRAM's sitting room. RAMZI is standing on a chair, refitting the top shelf of the wooden bookcase that holds a number of books, CDs and DVDs. Some books and other things have been put on the floor so that RAMZI can fix the shelf. RAMZI's tool box is also there. NADINE is watching him and trying to help.

RAMZI

If you don't mind me asking, Ms. Nadine, why are you still with him if he won't marry you and he doesn't even know how to use a hammer and a nail?!

NADINE

That's not fair, he doesn't have the time...

RAMZI

How long does it take?

NADINE

To get married or to fix a shelf?

RAMZI

Both.

NADINE

If you don't mind me saying, Mr. Ramzi... Look who's talking! Why didn't you get married?

RAMZI

I'm a special case! I told you that!

NADINE

Me too. And Akram.

RAMZI

Can you hold the shelf there for me please?

NADINE goes towards him and helps him to fix the shelf against the wall.

NADINE

I don't know why I'm getting all these things fixed, Akram might leave this place soon … If I hadn't already told you to come, I wouldn't have bothered you …

RAMZI

Really? You're leaving?

NADINE

Akram's going to work in Syria.

RAMZI

And he's taking you with him?

NADINE

I can't just drop everything and follow him!

RAMZI

Why not?

NADINE

Because!

RAMZI

Because you're not married!

NADINE

Oh my God! You're worse than my mother!

RAMZI

Your mother wants what's best for you …

NADINE

And what's best for a girl is to get married, isn't it?

RAMZI

What does he do?

NADINE
He works at the bank.

RAMZI
You work together?

NADINE
He's in a different branch. And he has a different job.

RAMZI
How's that?

NADINE
He's more numbers and money...

RAMZI
And you?

NADINE
I'm in human resources, so more with people...

RAMZI
That's what I thought!

NADINE
Really? What did you think?

RAMZI
That you don't look like your average bank employee.

NADINE
(*Laughing*) Why, what's wrong with bank employees?

RAMZI
Wrong? Nothing—what a life! Work, salary, bonus, a pension! God knows what else! Good for you! (*After making sure the shelf is firmly fixed*) That's sorted now, but don't put too many books on it. If you want, I could add a shelf on the wall to take some weight off the bookcase.

NADINE
We'll see, if we stay here... (*She checks the shelf to make sure it's firmly fixed,*

and looks at the bookcase.) Back when we were kids, my dad had a pistol he used to hide on the top shelf of the bookcase, behind the big books.

RAMZI
What kind of pistol was it, do you remember?

NADINE
Don't know. A small silver one. Mum hated guns, but dad used to tell her that this pistol was hers, in case she ever needed it, when he wasn't around.

RAMZI
In the War, every house had three or four guns, an automatic too!

NADINE
True. My dad used to have an automatic but mum didn't let him bring it into the house. Did you have one?

RAMZI
You bet! Still do!

NADINE
Have you ever killed anyone?

RAMZI
You're funny, you know.

NADINE
True, it's your job. You told me.

RAMZI
It's a bit difficult the first time, then you get used to it. Kill or be killed.

NADINE
Do you remember the first time?

RAMZI
The first time what?

NADINE
You killed someone!

RAMZI
Crystal clear.

NADINE
When was it?

RAMZI
Long time ago now ... Do you remember the Green Line? Or maybe you were too young ...

NADINE
I don't remember it but I know where it was ...

RAMZI
That's where it happened. I was seventeen or so, I used to go training with the lads in the neighborhood. They'd put bottles out so we could practice shooting them. They gave me a pistol and told me to shoot. I'd shoot at the bottle and hit it straight off. I was good at it because I had an air gun and used to like shooting birds. They were impressed and gave me a big rifle. It made it harder because the rifle whacks back into your shoulder when you pull the trigger. At first, it throws your whole body back. You've got to get used to it. I thought it was fun, and with practice I got pretty good at it. Then they started taking me with them to the front line. We were based in one building, and on the opposite side there was a building controlled by the Syrian army.

NADINE
What year was this?

RAMZI
When the Syrians came into Lebanon, '78. I'd go to the place we were based with the lads in the morning and I'd come back in the evening. Sometimes there'd be shooting and I'd shoot in the air, other times it would be calm, not a noise to be heard. One day, I remember well, I was strolling around the building, from floor to floor, there was no one there, nothing, it was calm, I was alone. I look out of the window and I see a Syrian soldier sweeping the terrace. He was as close as that building there. (*He points towards the window.*) Just calmly sweeping

away, taking his time. I stood and watched him. He must have been about eighteen, fair-skinned and sunburned. He was wearing slippers and a vest, as if he'd just woken up. Clearly, no one had warned him that he shouldn't go about all exposed like that. He must have just been some normal, low-ranking soldier they'd got to pick up rubbish and didn't care about. If I shoot, I'll hit him for sure, I can kill him on the spot. I thought about it. I looked at him and I felt sorry for him. I thought if I shoot him now, the others'll shoot back, it will be a big mess. If I leave him be, the day will go by, I'll go home, maybe he'll survive the War, go back to his country, back to his mum and his brothers and sisters. Let's just take it easy. When I went down and told my mates, they lost it—how could I have a Syrian soldier right there in front of me and not kill him? If he'd seen me, did I think he would have let me get away? We went back up to where I'd seen him. He was gone. We waited for him to come back, he didn't. We were about to go down and they all started making fun of me, telling me how I was such a coward, such an idiot. Suddenly someone came out. It wasn't him. I took aim and shot him dead.

NADINE
And what happened?

RAMZI
It all kicked off.

NADINE
And that Syrian, did you see him again?

RAMZI
No. You think he made it back home?

NADINE
I don't know.

SCENE FOURTEEN

NADINE is on the roof where ROBERT and RAMZI's flat is. She has RAMZI's tool box. It seems he forgot it at AKRAM's. The door is ajar. She knocks and no one answers. She knocks again. No answer. She pushes the door and goes in. No one is in the first room, where ROBERT usually stays. She goes into the second room. She sees RAMZI sleeping on the bed. He's lying curled up like a fetus, with his head buried in the covers. She can only see his neck and his hair from behind. She stays fixed to the spot and decides to wait for a bit. She sits down on the sofa in front of him. His shoes, black army Ranger boots, are on the floor by the bed. She stands up, she wants to wake him up, but she hesitates. Suddenly she lies down in the bed next to him. She holds him as if he were a small child. He carries on sleeping.

ACT TWO

SCENE ONE

AKRAM's bedroom. AKRAM is standing in front of a half-packed suitcase. We see NADINE standing in front of the wardrobe, helping him pack.

NADINE
(*Giving him a sweater*) Take this too, you'll need it and the color suits you.

AKRAM takes the sweater.

AKRAM
That's it. I've had enough of packing. I'll take what's left when I'm next back. What's the point carrying a heavy suitcase?

NADINE
We've packed everything you might need anyway. Let's put the stuff you don't want to take with you to Damascus to one side, so you can take it to your parents'.

AKRAM
(*Continuing to pack the bag*) There's no need to take stuff to my parents' yet! We still have two months of rent paid… Until the end of June!

NADINE
I wish we hadn't got the boiler put in the kitchen! What a waste! I've still got the receipt. The landlord should pay at least half of it.

AKRAM
I don't think he will.

NADINE
Ask him anyway!

AKRAM
He'll say, "You installed it to use it yourselves, and it wasn't necessary."

NADINE
But we hardly used it, and yes it was necessary!

AKRAM
Why are you so stressed about that boiler? Forget about it! (*Closing the suitcase*) Okay, we're done.

NADINE
What time are you leaving tomorrow?

AKRAM
Not too early. I don't want to get caught in traffic, about 11.

NADINE
Okay. I'm going to go now.

AKRAM
You're not going to sleep here? This is the last night…

NADINE
What do you mean last night? Aren't you coming back at the weekend, and every weekend?

AKRAM
(*Trying to soften her up*) The last night before I officially start my new job… You want to leave me all alone? (*He goes near her, she hugs him.*)

NADINE
You're a big boy now, you're a man, you just got an important job… And I'm tired and I've got a lot to do tomorrow…

AKRAM
I know you're angry with me because I took the job so quickly, and didn't give you any choice, but they needed someone at the branch straight away, and the money's good…

NADINE
I know, I know… It's done now! How many times have we talked about it?!

AKRAM
In four or five months I'll be able to afford a deposit for a flat. My dad will help too…

NADINE
Okay, okay…

We hear the sound of ROBERT*'s shouting coming from outside.*

ROBERT
Ta ta ta ta ta ta ta ta ta…

NADINE
Oh no, not today, Robert, not today! My head's about to explode!

She leaves the room.

SCENE TWO

Evening in a hotel room. NADINE *is lying in the bed. Her phone rings. She answers.*

NADINE

Hello ... yes mum ... No, I'm not sleeping, I'm just having a bit of a rest ... (RAMZI *comes out of the bathroom.* NADINE *motions to him to be quiet.*) No, I'm not ill, I'm fine, just tired from work ... Don't worry I'm keeping warm ... Yes ... Yes he's calling me ... Yes he's okay, he's happy ... I have no idea what he's eating! ... No, he doesn't know how to cook ... Yes, his mum gave him some food before he left ... He's not going to starve to death! It's not the desert you know! There must be a hundred restaurants there! ... Yes he'll be back next Friday ... I will ... Okay ... Fine, bye mum, bye. (*She hangs up.*) Just what I need! My mum nagging about what Akram's eating!

RAMZI

I'm impressed, though, you're such a good liar ...

NADINE

What should I do? Tell her the truth? ... Aren't you lying to anyone?

RAMZI

I don't have to. Robert couldn't care less where I sleep and when I get home ...

NADINE

I don't mean Robert ...

RAMZI

I know. I still don't have to. I'm not married.

NADINE

I'm not married either!

RAMZI

Near enough ... I guess it would've been better if you were. There's nothing more straightforward than married women. They don't give you any headaches.

NADINE
So I'm giving you a headache?

RAMZI
(*He gets close to her, trying to avoid the seriousness of the conversation.*) You're giving me … a heartache! How about that? Better than a headache?

NADINE
Speaking of headaches, why was Robert shouting the other day?

RAMZI
When?

NADINE
A couple of days ago, the night before Akram left … Friday evening.

RAMZI
How would I know? I wasn't at home. On Fridays I go and play poker with the lads.

NADINE
The ones you watch the War with, the Iraq War …

RAMZI
What?

NADINE
That's what Robert told me when I was waiting for you at your place.

RAMZI
He talks a lot of rubbish, and you keep on chatting to him …

NADINE
And he said you're from Zahlé …

RAMZI
Not true. He must have heard it somewhere.

NADINE
And the time before, he said his mum died when they were giving her a C-section when she was having you, because you weighed eleven pounds…

RAMZI
He's funny, my brother… He must have seen something on TV. Mum died fifteen years ago. She used to live with him. She was the one who wouldn't let him be sent to the asylum. She even kept that flat for him. So I'm actually a guest at his place.

NADINE
Are you going to go away again?

RAMZI
I haven't made up my mind yet. When I got back, two months ago, I was exhausted. I couldn't stand Iraq or Americans anymore. But they pay good money, 5,000 dollars a month. How would I make that here?

NADINE
I just want to understand how you ended up in Iraq!

RAMZI
But I already told you! You really think the Americans would let their soldiers die, let them be hunted down like birds? There are men from all over the world fighting for them out there!

NADINE
Mercenaries, you mean…

RAMZI
Yes, mercenaries… Human shields… From Colombia, Mexico, Nepal, France, from the US too… But these fighters are even stronger than the American army! They're experienced. The Europeans get paid ridiculous amounts of money. Some of them get 10,000 dollars a day!

NADINE
Woah. Ten thousand?

RAMZI
Yes, honest! A French guy I met when I first went there stayed for two

years then left. He made loads of money. He worked with me guarding convoys. Now he's back home working as a bodyguard for some artist or actor ... I liked him a lot ... We'd be three or four in the car, he'd put music on and start singing ... Then we'd take it in turns to pick a song, and he'd sing along, to any song, even Arabic ... You know what's the most important thing when you're on the road there?

NADINE
What?

RAMZI
To be faster than the sniper. We drive 300km an hour! And we don't always make it ... I've been in loads of cars that got hit, the doors full of holes, the windscreen shattered. And then there are the ones I was with who died ... And the explosions ... In Iraq, every time you put your head down on your pillow and go to sleep, you've cheated death for a day. "Une journée en enfer,"[9] that's what the French guy used to say. He couldn't take more than two years. He said he wanted to live!

NADINE
What about you, don't you want to live?

RAMZI
We all want to live.

NADINE
Stay here then ...

RAMZI
If I go back, you can come with me, I'll take you for a walk down al-Mutannabi Street. You'll love it! Books! Everywhere! On the ground, in little stalls, old ones, new ones, people selling, people buying, people browsing ...

NADINE
Yeah, that street's famous, I've heard about it before. But maybe let's give it a miss for now, just in case we get killed by a bomb ...

---

9 In French in the original ("a day in hell").

RAMZI
You're Druze, if you die you'll be reincarnated.[10] I'm the one who'd be gone for good!

NADINE
Let's not take the risk, then. I don't feel like being reincarnated right now anyway, I'm only just starting to get to grips with this life ... What are the women there like? Are they pretty?

RAMZI
Yes they are. And they're always well turned out. Eyeliner and lipstick ...

NADINE
Don't they wear the veil?

RAMZI
The veil and the black abaya! So what? It's sexier with the veil ... And some don't wear it. The way they look at you ...

NADINE
So that's how it is! Come on, let's go ...

RAMZI
Where? Baghdad?

NADINE
No, home. Up you get.

RAMZI
Why? We've got till tomorrow morning!

NADINE
You'll take me home early in the morning so I can get to work?

RAMZI
I'll take you whenever you want, wherever you want!

10 Druze believe in reincarnation.

SCENE THREE

AKRAM*'s apartment. The doorbell rings.* NADINE *comes out of the kitchen and opens the door. It's* RAMZI.

NADINE
(*Surprised*) What are you doing here? Come in, quick.

RAMZI *comes in,* NADINE *shuts the door, he hugs her.*

RAMZI
I missed you.

NADINE
Didn't we say we'd see each other on Tuesday? What's going on?

RAMZI
I miss you so much, and I knew you'd be here today.

NADINE
Did anyone see you coming up?

RAMZI
So what if they did? They'd think I'd come to fix something.

NADINE
You can't stay long. Akram'll be here soon.

RAMZI
Come round to mine for a bit this evening.

NADINE
I can't.

RAMZI
Tell him you've got to go to the shop.

NADINE
I really can't.

RAMZI
Yes you can!

NADINE
Okay, I'll see what I can do. Please go now though.

RAMZI
You'll come?

NADINE
I don't know!

SCENE FOUR

The hotel room where RAMZI *and* NADINE *meet. They are in bed, it looks like they have just had sex.*

NADINE
I've missed you so much. And even when I'm with you now, I still miss you. (RAMZI *smiles.*) Sometimes I miss you like you're someone else, someone I've loved for years.

RAMZI *doesn't answer, he looks happy with what she's saying. He is holding her in his arms. Silence.*

NADINE
Ramzi ...

RAMZI
Yes ...

NADINE
I want to leave him ... I want to leave Akram.

RAMZI
(*He sits up.*) Are you asking me or telling me?

NADINE
I'm telling you. I've made up my mind. Why would I stay with him?

RAMZI
Don't you want to get married?

NADINE
But I'm cheating on him! I'm in bed with you right now, how could I marry him?

RAMZI
Does he know you're cheating on him?

NADINE
No, of course not! He can sense that I've changed; he thinks I'm

angry with him because he asked to be transferred to Syria. But he definitely doesn't know.

RAMZI
Could any man not know?! Are you still sleeping with him?

NADINE
I can't believe you're asking me that!

RAMZI
If he doesn't know and hasn't noticed anything, it means you're still sleeping with him!

NADINE
I just told you he thinks I'm angry with him! And every time I make up an excuse! Is that all you care about? Whether I'm still sleeping with him or not? If it's bothering you that much, why don't you ask me to leave him? Why don't you tell me you want me for yourself? Why are you letting me decide for myself?

RAMZI
Because I'm not the one who wants to marry you, he's the one who wants to marry you. I can't take on that responsibility.

NADINE
What responsibility? Who said I wanted to marry you?

RAMZI
If you want to leave him, leave him, but don't do it for me...

NADINE *gets up and starts to get dressed, talking to herself angrily as she does so.*

NADINE
I can't believe it, I honestly can't believe it, "I don't want to marry you"... "I can't take on the responsibility"... Who asked you to take on any responsibility? Who asked you for anything in the first place?

RAMZI
Nadine, calm down, listen to me, you think I haven't thought about

it? Okay. We meet. We talk. We make love. We have a few nice hours together. And where are we going? Nowhere. I've noticed that you're getting quite attached to me...

NADINE

Oh. And you couldn't care less. You send me 100 messages a day, when Akram's here you go crazy, you're dying to know if I'm still sleeping with him, and it's me who's getting attached to you!

RAMZI

Okay, fine. I'm attached to you too. Really quite attached, actually. Happy? We'll stay like this for two, three, four months, a year. Then what? We're getting attached for nothing.

NADINE

I don't care. I don't care if I get attached to you and then we split up. Nothing lasts forever anyway.

RAMZI

Would you stop being so dramatic? Why do you want to leave Akram? He loves you and he wants to marry you and he's Druze like you!

NADINE

I want to leave him because I don't feel anything for him anymore, because I think about you all the time, I want to be with you all the time, I want to talk to you all the time. When we're about to see each other I just can't wait for it to happen. I want to leave him because after we've been together, I'm smiling and laughing for two whole days and I can put up with how stupid and annoying people are. Even the traffic doesn't bother me. I want to leave him because with you I don't feel alone, because I can talk to you about anything and you always listen, because when you look at me it's like you can't see anyone else, and you'd do anything to stay with me for one more minute. (*Silence.*) I've thought about it too, and I know it won't work. But I couldn't care less. I think what we have with each other is at least worth a try.

RAMZI

You're right. We do have something. And if I could, I'd see you every day too and sleep beside you every night. But these moments you're talking about, they're a truce, a cease fire. Life's not like that ... You know that ... You're not getting any younger ... A year from now, you'd want to get married and have children ... What would you tell your parents then? I want to marry a Christian who's 16 years older than me, used to be in the Lebanese Forces, and is now a professional killer who works in Iraq and fixes lifts?

NADINE
You're the one being dramatic. You even came up with some imaginary scenario! Who told you I wanted to get married in the first place?

RAMZI
You'll decide you want to any day now—you're a woman. If I wanted to get married, I would've done it a long time ago. This is my life; I don't take responsibility for anything or anyone. Today I'm here, tomorrow I'm gone. That's what I got used to do. That's how I grew up.

NADINE
Obviously! Because you don't have any feelings! What would you expect from a Lebanese Forces fighter! A war criminal!

RAMZI
You knew that from the beginning, why did you come up to mine and sleep in my bed?

NADINE
Yeah, cuz you really hated that!

RAMZI
If your boyfriend knew you were sleeping with me, what would he do? What would your parents do? They'd come down and slit my throat? Or your dad would lock me in the basement and take the skin off my dick! I managed to get away from you lot in the war, and you followed me here?

NADINE
I've had enough of this "you lot," "you Druze"! What does it have to

do with me? Did I ever say "you lot" to you? You were the ones who started it in the first place! You, you, what were you doing in the Mountain? Didn't they make you go up there to kill? You keep on saying: "You slaughtered, you did this, you threw the bodies in the well ..." Because you lot didn't do anything! You didn't kidnap anyone at checkpoints, and you didn't massacre anyone in Kfarmatta, in Bennay, in Abey, in Brih!

RAMZI

Who started it? Who killed the people in the church in Brih and didn't even let their families bury them in '77?

NADINE

I don't know! Not me! Wasn't there! (*Silence.*) "You, you, you, you lot ..." Our dead bodies weren't left lying on the ground? We were defending our land too!

RAMZI

Of course! That's how the Druze defend their land! They cut their neighbors' throats and take their houses! Yeah ... It's your right, it's your right ... It's just self-defence ... If one of you dies, you kill 100, 200, whole villages! Men, women, children, it doesn't matter! What matters is to kill! To get revenge! You were always like that and you always will be! And you won! Happy? The Mountain's yours! Enjoy it! I only wish you'd stay there!

And for your information, seeing as you're obviously such an expert on the war archives, what you did in the Mountain is called genocide, not self-defense.

Reconciliation, they say, reconciliation[11] ... Lies, lies, just a bunch of lies ... Words they distract people with between one war and the next ...

(*Silence.*) Why don't you leave me alone, Nadine? What do you want from me? You want to apply the "coexistence formula" with me?[12]

11 In reference to "The Reconciliation Agreement" previously mentioned.

12 The expression "coexistence formula" is often used in press and speeches. It's a fundamental principle of the Lebanese constitution, and refers to the fact that Lebanese citizens live together despite great sectarian differences.

You know what your problem is? The books and the films that broke the shelf ... They damaged your brain ... Take my advice: keep your feet on the ground.

SCENE FIVE

ROBERT's room on the roof. NADINE is sitting in front of him. RAMZI is sleeping in the next room where the TV is on as usual.

ROBERT
Wake him up, wake him up.

NADINE
No, it's fine. We'll sit here together, us two, he'll wake up on his own.

ROBERT
Ramzi, Ramzi!

RAMZI
(*Sleeping*) Let me sleep, Robbie!

NADINE
Let him sleep, he must be tired.

ROBERT
It's better for him to sleep. Is Leila still at the ministry?

NADINE
Who's Leila?

ROBERT
Your sister!

NADINE
My sister's not called Leila. (*Correcting herself*) No, she quit.

ROBERT
Do you still go to France?

NADINE
Not much.

ROBERT
Not much, not much, not always ... (*He starts muttering.*)

RAMZI*'s voice comes from inside.*

RAMZI
Nadine, is that you?

NADINE
Yes, it's me.

RAMZI
Come in. (NADINE *goes into the next room and remains standing.*)

NADINE
I called you twice. Why aren't you answering my calls?

RAMZI
I'm busy.

NADINE
I miss you.

RAMZI
Sit down.

NADINE
I don't want to stay here. Can we go somewhere and talk?

RAMZI
What's left to talk about? We said everything there is to say. If we're going to go somewhere, it won't be to talk.

NADINE
(*She looks at him angrily.*) So that's what really matters to you?

RAMZI
I've never liked talking anyway. You might be the woman I've talked to most in my whole life. And look where it got us ...

NADINE
Don't you miss me?

RAMZI
Yes I do. A lot. But what difference does it make? It's not working. (*Silence.*) If you just want to have sex, no problem. If you want to drag me into endless discussions and stories, forget about it.

NADINE
Why are you talking to me like this?

RAMZI
Because this is how I am. You said it—an ex-militia guy and a war criminal. And the talking's all pointless.

SCENE SIX

AKRAM's apartment. AKRAM and NADINE are in the sitting room. They look like they've just finished eating the meal NADINE usually prepares before AKRAM comes home.

AKRAM
When did you do the Canada application?

NADINE
Four years ago, straight after the July War.

AKRAM
Why did you never tell me about it?

NADINE
I didn't tell anyone! Just my work friends who I applied with. It was their idea anyway. We were feeling pretty desperate after the War and we all applied together.

AKRAM
You've been working on this application for four years, and you haven't mentioned it once?!

NADINE
I applied before I met you. And do you have any idea what it's like to apply to immigrate to Canada? You send in a few forms and forget about it. They send you an update every year or so! Besides, you don't even like to travel, and I thought fine, we'll stay here together, I might as well not mention it...

AKRAM
You're right. I don't like to travel, and I couldn't care less about Canada!

NADINE
But now my application's been accepted!

AKRAM
So what if it's been accepted! You want to leave?

NADINE
I can go and visit and then come back, see whether it suits me...

AKRAM
And if it suits you, you'll leave!

NADINE
You'll come with me then! We'll get married, you'll do your papers and we'll go together...

AKRAM
I'm never going to emigrate. You know that.

NADINE
My love, getting Canadian nationality would sort our whole lives out for us! Who turns down a Canadian passport? Don't you remember how the boats came and rescued the people with foreign passports in the July War? Did anyone care about us? No, no one! A human being with a Lebanese passport is worth nothing. They could do 500 air strikes right over your head every night, kill 5000 people every day, no one would bat an eyelid! Canada is an advanced country, with lots of job opportunities. We'll go, we'll start a new life, we'll get the nationality and if we want to come back, we'll come back!

AKRAM
What about your job? My job? Your parents? Life?

NADINE
What job? What parents? What life? What are you talking about? Is there actually anything real and worthwhile that's keeping us here? What's the most we can hope for? I could get a salary of two or three thousand dollars, working a hundred times as hard! If we do manage to buy a flat, we'll be paying off the mortgage for the next seventy years. That's if we do manage. And what's this life that we'd be missing? Our parents meddling in everything we do? Or the restaurant where we go and smoke shisha once a month and sing

along to a bit of Abdel Halim and Fayruz? We can still come back for the summer and smoke and sing and eat! If the Arab tourists leave us any space, that is. It's so kind of them to bring us their money, their traffic, their rubbish! Lebanon, a piece of heaven on earth, the Gulf's brothel, the place where all the neighbors come to let off steam. Anyway, this country's always been on the edge. Any excuse and we'll start killing each other. We may as well all die, it wouldn't be a big loss. I wish Ahmadinejad would drop one of his nuclear bombs on Israel, maybe we'd blow up too, and this whole region would be wiped off the face of the earth.

AKRAM

What's wrong with you Nadine? What's going on? I don't understand what's going on inside your head anymore!

NADINE

Nothing's wrong. I just want a boat to come and wait for me if there's ever a war again. I want someone to care about me.

AKRAM

I don't want to go to Canada. This is our country and it's always been like this. Even if there is another war, I'm not leaving.

SCENE SEVEN

ROBERT and RAMZI's flat on the roof. The door is half open. NADINE knocks.

ROBERT
Come in.

NADINE
(*As she's coming in*) How are you, Robert?

ROBERT
Fine and you two?

NADINE
Fine, everything's good.

ROBERT
Ramzi's not in.

NADINE
Can I stay with you a little while, till he comes back?

ROBERT
Make yourselves at home. Hi! What's up?

NADINE
I'm going to Canada.

ROBERT
On Middle East?

NADINE
I don't know which airline. I haven't booked yet.

ROBERT
Booked ... book ... I like books.

NADINE
Really? Me too.

ROBERT
Those shoes you're wearing, those heels are crepe.

NADINE
Exactly, so I don't slip. They're very comfortable, I walk a lot.

ROBERT
Crepe.

NADINE
Crepe.

ROBERT
Crepe … (*He mutters something incomprehensible. It is as if he's playing with words.*)

NADINE
(*She watches him*) Do you want anything from Canada if I come back?

ROBERT
No thanks. Why did you trouble yourselves? You're most welcome.

RAMZI *comes in.*

RAMZI
Nadine?

NADINE
Oh here you are. I was about to leave.

RAMZI
What is it? Did the boiler blow up?

NADINE
(*Smiling*) No, I've come to say goodbye.

RAMZI
That's it? You're leaving the neighborhood?

NADINE
Not just the neighborhood. I'm going to Canada.

RAMZI
Oh. Good luck. Are you going to get married there?

NADINE
No. We broke up.

RAMZI
Oh.

NADINE
Akram doesn't want to go to Canada.

RAMZI
Why not? They say Canada's nice.

NADINE
He doesn't want to. Are you well?

RAMZI
Yes, thanks.

NADINE
Are you going back to Iraq?

RAMZI
I don't know. Maybe. Haven't decided yet.

NADINE
Can I ask you something?

RAMZI
Whatever you like.

NADINE
Can you tell me how Robert got to be like this?

RAMZI
Okay, I'll tell you. (*Quietly*) Come inside. It's better not to talk in front of him, he'll get upset. (*To Robert*) I'm going to turn the TV on for you Robbie.

He turns on the TV. ROBERT *sits in front of it as usual and smokes.* RAMZI *and* NADINE *go into the next room.* NADINE *sits on the sofa and* RAMZI *sits in front of her on the bed.*

At the start of the War, in '76, Robert was fighting here on the Green Line in Horsh Tabet. You know the main road between the Seasweet[13] and the Levant hospital? That was the green line in the battle of Tel el-Zaatar. The exact place where the fighting happened is now a park, the Horsh Tabet Park. We used to live there. The battle happened right next to our house. He'd go out to fight and then come back home.

NADINE
Do you remember him then?

RAMZI
Course I do! He was strong, he played football, he was always well turned out! One day he was out there with his friends and they got shot. The shots were coming from a building and he shot straight back at it. The guy who was shooting fell on top of him. He was Somali. You know in the War, there were those tall Somalis who the Palestinians brought in to fight with them ...

NADINE
Yes ...

RAMZI
He came home upset. Then one morning, one or two years later, he woke up and he wasn't the same. He's been like you see him now ever since. At first he didn't shout, though. Now he's more and more out of it.

NADINE
Did he tell you his friends were shot?

13 Famous pastry shop in Lebanon.

RAMZI
He didn't tell us anything. People started talking, that's how we found out.

NADINE
Did you take him to the doctor?

RAMZI
To all the best doctors!

NADINE
And what did they say?

RAMZI
Now his doctor says he'll stay like this, and he'll get worse as he gets older.

NADINE
Does he never talk about the War?

RAMZI
No.

NADINE
So he's been out of it for almost 35 years!

RAMZI
Since '76.

NADINE
Do you think it was more because his friends died or because he killed the Somali?

RAMZI
(*Sarcastically*) Ask him.

ROBERT *starts shouting.*

ROBERT
Ta ta ta ta ta ta ta ta ta ta ...

RAMZI

Ah. He must have heard us talking about him. That's what happens whenever anyone talks about the War in front of him...

NADINE

Sometimes I feel like shouting with him...

RAMZI

What for? He shouts for all of us.

ROBERT

Ta ta ta ta ta ta ta ta ta ta...

ACT THREE

SCENE ONE

Four years later. We see NADINE *coming down the stairs that lead to* ROBERT *and* RAMZI*'s flat. Then she enters the small shop that's next to the building where they live. The* SHOPKEEPER *is busy placing some goods on the shelves.* NADINE *looks at the boxes that have fruits and vegetables in them.*

NADINE
Hello.

SHOPKEEPER
Hello.

NADINE
Tell me, don't you sell Egyptian mangoes anymore?

SHOPKEEPER
(*He looks at her.*) Yes I do. But they're not in season.

NADINE
(*She smiles at him.*) Do you remember me? I had friends living in the building behind, I used to come to your shop a lot …

SHOPKEEPER
Yes, yes … It's been a while since we've seen you around! Two, three years?!

NADINE
Four, to be precise.

SHOPKEEPER
Oh! That long? Time flies … So? Did your friends leave the neighborhood?

NADINE
Yes and I did too. I live in Canada now.

SHOPKEEPER
Good for you! The people who managed to get out of this country are the lucky ones ... What a relief!

NADINE
(*Smiling*) You'd think so! But it's hard ...

SHOPKEEPER
Nothing's harder than living here, believe me!

NADINE
You may be right ...

SHOPKEEPER
I am right and you know it.

NADINE
I'm not going to lie to you, the country feels like it's changed, and not for the better ... The noise, the crowd, the stress. It's like people can't stand each other ... I don't know if I'm just not used to it anymore, or if things really are bleak ...

SHOPKEEPER
Things really are bleak. I'm telling you. Even just the Syrians are enough for us to deal with. They're half of the population now ... (*Sighing*) Whether it's peacetime or wartime in Syria, we are always in trouble. We're truly blessed!

NADINE
Even the neighborhood has changed. They're putting up so many new buildings!

SHOPKEEPER
More than you could count! The noise is unbearable!

NADINE
And you don't need any extra noise here! Is Robert still shouting?

SHOPKEEPER
He died. Poor Robert! About a year and a half ago.

NADINE
Ohh! What happened?

SHOPKEEPER
Heart attack. He kept on smoking and shouting till his heart gave up... God rest his soul...

NADINE
...And now his brother lives alone in the flat?

SHOPKEEPER
Ramzi's in the US now!

NADINE
Really?

SHOPKEEPER
Yes! Two or three years ago, he got badly injured in Iraq. His whole arm was smashed. I don't know whether it was amputated or not in the end, but he couldn't move it anymore... The Americans gave him one-hundred-thousand dollars' compensation, citizenship, and there you go...

NADINE
...And do you have new neighbors now up on the roof?

SHOPKEEPER
A Syrian family's renting the place. (*Silence.*) If you're still here in a month or a month and a half, come by. It'll be mango season.

NADINE
I wish I could. I'm going back in two weeks.

SHOPKEEPER
Never mind. Safe travels. Don't they have mangoes in Canada?

NADINE
They've got everything, but fruit tastes different here ... Plums, grapes, apples... They don't taste of anything... Even the trees there smell of nothing.

SHOPKEEPER
But these are Egyptian mangoes we're talking about!

NADINE
So what?! Egyptian mangoes in Lebanon taste different!

SHOPKEEPER
Next time make sure you visit when they're in season.

NADINE
You'll still be here?

SHOPKEEPER
(*Opens his arms in a gesture signifying that he's unable to give any answer.*) Who knows?

BRAVEHEART

by Wael Kadour

translated by Clem Naylor

ON *BRAVEHEART*

Wael Kadour's *Braveheart* vibrates between concentric circles. The play's gaze first pins itself to Aline, a refugee and aspiring novelist. The circles quickly turn to smoke rings; audiences waft through the pleasures of indeterminant time, slithering in, slithering out. All at once: circle becomes panopticon becomes prism.

Aline is vying for a publishing grant. Muhammad is advising her. They read excerpts of her latest project. They disagree over style. Truth and fiction distort as they both muscle their way inside their literary proxies, prompting debate over the who, the how, the when. I first read this play in the dark, just as Muhammad reads Aline's various drafts. Nighttime appeals to my most engaged state—the reader as damnable participant. A play's plot becomes a dispatch in nocturne. *Braveheart*'s characters implicate one another, stoke paranoia, and call forth the question: how might a writer facilitate control through the vehicle of literary fantasy?

Aline drills, "I'll always be stuck in a spiral of mirrors."

Parsing through Kadour's monologues, I sometimes forget to breathe. I suspect these characters do the same. The author has capitalized on the Droste effect; recursive threats have everyone acting as echo or phantom. Muhammad and Aline have arrived in a new country; they write to retrieve memory. But did they meet at a language course? Did they meet under more insidious circumstances? Who is a martyr? A whistleblower? A member of the secret police? Who interrogates whom? And who will stay the night? Kadour is winking. Time is folding. As temporal dimensions shift, characters become phantoms of a still-suspended future.

When I spoke to Kadour about his play, he highlighted the recent Koblenz trials in Germany that spanned 2020 to 2022. These proceedings saw the first guilty verdicts of two former Syrian intelligence officers for their perpetration of torture, murder, sexual violence. "This might be the only trial we have in the Syrian political context," Kadour informs me. I feel the weight of a devastation recognized. There is a light seeded by this moment of accountability, accompanied by a left-over dread from such a fleeting sense of justice. Kadour's characters' demand to be witnessed elevates tenfold.

In the play's most sober gesture, Aline climbs a chair to wrap a plastic bag over the flat's smoke detector. I see this as the character and playwright's shared interception. They suffocate the machine-body, the punitive spectator, to indulge in a brief window of respite—if only for the sake of an indoor cigarette. *Braveheart* is simultaneously a story of political injustice, as well as an artist's retching. Kadour has beckoned us into this theatre of facsimile. I encourage readers to remain porous, activate their subconscious, flay their hearts open, and stare beyond the balcony.

— Lucas Baisch, December 1, 2023

CHARACTERS

MUHAMMAD

ALINE

ACT ONE

ALINE

Yes, of course.
A lot.
I'm still afraid of him. I hate him.
When I was in Lebanon I dreamt about him a lot.
He's suffocating me.
To be honest that time in Lebanon was totally shit.
Then as time went by I slowly started forgetting about him.
And then when I came here I completely forgot about him.
But I got depressed.
I feel like being here and being safe has unleashed every fear you could imagine inside me.
I was hooked on hash for a long time. 24/7.
Then I started having panic attacks.
Not too bad to begin with, then they got worse. Then the suicidal thoughts started.
That was when I started treatment. Medication and therapy.
Till I started getting a bit better.
Then I could start living again, and working, and learning the language.
That was my best time here.
But what's happening at home meant I was always …
Stuck.
It keeps me going round in circles. I get a bit better and then I get a bit worse.
Never ending circles. They just get bigger. The more time you spend in them, the bigger they get!

I happen to be in touch with a friend of mine.
He tells me that that person got out of the country and came to Europe and got asylum.
Just a rumor.
But since then I've been …
Honestly I don't know the word for what I've been.
I was thinking that I'd finally got a new life.

Without him.
And without all the past.
But then I found myself constantly thinking about him.
I found myself asking about him. I tried to find out what he was up to.
Before I left the station he gave me his phone number and asked me to call him if I needed anything.
I found the number and called it but it was out of service.
No one knew anything about him.
There's no trace of him. Like he didn't exist.
Some people said he was still where he was, some people said he'd been killed.
Some people said he probably had left the country.
But no one could say where he had gone to.

I saw him.
I was on the tram and I saw him walking in the street.
I thought I was imagining it but it was so realistic.
I told myself it could be because I was thinking about him so much.
I still don't know if I imagined it or not.
Probably I did imagine it.
What would bring him to a small town like this?!

The panic attacks started again.
I started on the medication again.

I started walking in the street where he was in case I saw him again.
I started imagining him all over the place. On the bus, in the street, in the market.
But I can't say for sure I was actually seeing him.
The first time it was really realistic, but it didn't happen so clearly again.
When I saw him again later, it was always in places where it was hard to check.
Just glimpses.
In a busy market or on the tram coming the other way or out of my window at home, walking in a crowd.

I became convinced that he was actually here, and that he might be living close by.

Then my imagination moved from outside the flat to inside.
Sometimes I'd be eating and look up and see him sitting in front of me.
And sometimes I'd imagine him standing on the balcony or sitting on the sofa or even having a shower.
Like he was living with me.
I started seeing him a lot in my dreams.
And when I opened up my eyes in the night, I'd see him lying next to me.

MUHAMMAD
What dreams?

ALINE
It's one dream that more or less repeats, but the details change.
Always at home.
Every time it looks different or he's doing something different.
I see him and he sees me. He speaks. And then he kills me.

MUHAMMAD
What does he say?

ALINE
I always forget what he says. But I'm sure every time he's saying something different. He's saying strange things and sometimes he goes on talking and I keep on watching him until he stops.
I'm just listening to him in silence.
And every time when he stops talking and goes quiet, I wake up.

MUHAMMAD
Then why did you say he kills you at the end of every dream?

ALINE
Because every time I wake up I have this feeling that I am dead.

MUHAMMAD
Can I say something?
What you just told me would be perfect for the novel.

ALINE

It's not going to be a novel.
I don't know what it's going to be.

MUHAMMAD

It doesn't matter.
What matters is that I wish you could write exactly what you just said.

ALINE

You mean try to work more on what I'm imagining?

MUHAMMAD

Yes.
Write from where you got to.
I mean the moment you saw him clearly for the first time and it was really realistic.
And then describe the other times you saw him and how you can't tell if they're real or imagined.
I mean you started seeing him a lot, and we don't know anymore when it was real and when it was an illusion.
It could be it really was real the first time.
A coincidence that never happened again.
A coincidence that happened and then your mind got stuck and you imagined seeing him again and again.

ALINE

To begin with I'll think what I'm seeing is an illusion, then little by little we'll find out it's not. I'm not imagining things, and that person who I think I'm imagining is an actual real person, he's the person who interrogated me and tortured me and he really came here to Europe and claimed asylum and ended up living in the same town as me.

MUHAMMAD

No. Don't try to answer that question. Stay lost between reality and illusion.

ALINE
But I have to know.

MUHAMMAD
Why do you want to know?

ALINE
So I can relax. So I can get on with my life.
I report him to the police and he's caught and he goes to court.

MUHAMMAD
And that's how justice is done!

ALINE
Yes, at least partially.

MUHAMMAD
But now it's turned into something else. Now you've stopped writing and started judging.
The good thing about what you're writing is that you're a victim, lost between reality and illusion, who doesn't know how to get on with her life because the past keeps attacking her. Stay where you are and work on how you can put it into writing.

ALINE
I don't want to stay where I am, Muhammad.
I don't want to.
Why is it a problem if I manage to achieve in my writing the thing I can't achieve in reality?
The shadow that is chasing me and suffocating me in my life I want to trap it inside my writing and get rid of it.

MUHAMMAD
I don't know if that will do you any good, to be honest.
It would be great if a chance sighting could lead you to the person who interrogated you and tortured you in a country where you can take him to court, but it's more or less impossible and if it did happen then it would be better if it happened in real life.

ALINE
Maybe you're right
The idea is really nice but only if it actually happens in real life.
But what good does it do if it happens in fiction?

MUHAMMAD
None.

ALINE
Exactly. None.

Silence.

I've got to go back.

MUHAMMAD
Let me take you.

ALINE
Don't worry about that. I'd like to go for a walk.

MUHAMMAD
Okay I won't take you, but I will come downstairs because I want a cigarette.

She looks up to where a smoke alarm is.

ALINE
Do you have a plastic bag?

She pulls over a chair and climbs onto it, with MUHAMMAD *watching.*

MUHAMMAD *hands her the bag.*

ALINE *wraps the alarm with a plastic bag and ties it tightly.*

She climbs down from the chair.

She takes a cigarette from MUHAMMAD*'s pack.*

She puts it in her mouth and lights it, to MUHAMMAD*'s astonishment.*

What if… What if I got him to help me?

MUHAMMAD
I don't understand.

ALINE
I see him. I remember him. But instead of reporting him to the police, I'm going to offer him a deal.
I ask him to tell me his story. He admits everything. He answers all my questions and in return I leave him alone.

MUHAMMAD
Nice idea but I don't think he'd agree.
There's no way he'd trust you.

ALINE
He wouldn't have a choice.

MUHAMMAD
He could run away. He could kill you or he could hurt you, but he's definitely not going to sit there telling you everything he's done while you write it all down in a book, when you could always change your mind and do him over.

ALINE
Wherever he escapes to, he'd be caught. And the idea that he'd hurt me—he wouldn't do it here. Very difficult.

MUHAMMAD
Okay maybe you're right. But in any case he won't trust you. And if there's no trust, he won't tell you the truth about himself.
He'll lie. And you'll know he's lying.
You'll each just be waiting for the other one to betray you. A deal wouldn't work. Trust me.

ALINE
You're right. Maybe I should stop thinking because I'm not coming

up with anything good.
Alright I'll put the application in like this, and if I don't get the grant then whatever. Just another failure.
I'm used to it.

ALINE *starts to leave;* MUHAMMAD *stays where he is.*

ALINE *approaches* MUHAMMAD *and hugs him.*

They hug for a long time. They move away from each other slowly.

ALINE *leaves.*

MUHAMMAD *stays where he is behind the door for a little time. It looks like he can't move away.*

After a few seconds, there's some loud banging on the door. MUHAMMAD *rushes to open the door.*

ALINE *rushes in.*

ALINE

If I want to meet him then I have to not know him.
I mean, he's a former member of the secret police and he's come here under a false identity, and I'm me—a girl who was in a secret police station—but we don't know each other. I mean, he's not the same person I told you about.
I know, you're going to ask me how I know who he is.
And the answer is that I don't need to know to start with.
The opposite actually—I need to not know.
Maybe I'll feel something strange about him but there's no way I can know or even have a suspicion.
I mean it's impossible for the idea to occur to me.
We'll meet by chance. We'll get to introduce ourselves just like any two people from the same country in a small town.
I'll tell him my story but he won't tell me his. I mean he won't tell me the truth about himself, obviously. He'll tell me something else.

He'll say what he's said about himself to people here.
And that's how the relationship will go.
He'll know I'm writing something and he'll read what I've written and tell me what he thinks about it.
Just a total stranger who will appear in the final act and start reading what I've written.
Or maybe I only start with the writing then.
Maybe I love him.
Maybe we live with each other.
Maybe he'll even help me finish what I'm writing.

ALINE *goes towards* MUHAMMAD *and kisses him on the lips.*

ACT TWO

MUHAMMAD is reading/speaking, not ALINE.
There is no mistake in the names of the characters.

MUHAMMAD

Act Two.
It's like I'm living with someone who doesn't exist.
He has this amazing ability to move about without making a sound.
Completely silent.
Suddenly I find him making the food and cleaning the house and washing the dishes and getting things.
How he's doing all this without me noticing I don't know!
Maybe because I'm so busy writing and thinking. Maybe that's why I don't notice him moving much.
Sometimes I jump when I see him.
Because he's here with me at the moment he's helping me more than I expected.
Our relationship developed quickly. I don't know what happened. I found myself kissing him like I hadn't kissed anyone else before.
And then everything happened unplanned. Everything happened by itself. Suddenly I found him in my life.

He can't oppose me in any way.
Not once has he done anything I don't want. Not once has he annoyed me or misled me. The nicest possible person.
The day proceeds at the rhythm I choose. And sometimes he knows what I want or what's on my mind before I even say it.
As if he can read my mind.

Food, for example.
I don't know how in such a short time he got to know what I like and don't like.
He prepares food with the flavours I like. The right amount of salt.
The right cooking time. The right portion size. The right time of day.
Everything is strangely perfect and well-organized. It all happens so

smoothly and without me really knowing how.

He doesn't call anyone and no one calls him. His mobile is always far away from him. Always on silent.
Like he doesn't know anyone. He's not on any social media. He doesn't have any accounts on anything.

There's one situation where he turns 180 degrees and turns into someone totally different.
When we have sex.
That gentle, quiet person turns into someone totally different.
Without me knowing how, it's him who decides when we're going to have sex and where and in what way.
He can make me completely surrender myself to him.
He takes control of every detail and every step.
Even if I'm not really in the mood for sex, he knows exactly how to make me want him.
Even this didn't happen suddenly.
Little by little and time after time I started to notice that he was in control of everything.
He does this with no violence or coercion.
He's impulsive and he's agile in a way that means I can't tell where he's going to move next. So I gradually give myself to him. He moves me. He directs me. He controls the rhythm and the position and the speed and the number of times and where and when ... It's amazing!

He started being distracted.
Like his mind was somewhere else.
I'm talking about a few seconds, nothing more than that.
And not every day.
I could feel him moving away. Just a sense, nothing more, but I could feel it.
And he knew I could feel it.
But neither of us said anything about it.
I occupied myself more with writing and he occupied himself more with looking after me.

I forgot to say something important about him. He's a very amusing person.

Often he says things that get me in fits of laughter. And usually he actually isn't trying to make me laugh. But when he's just telling a story, he does it in a way that gets me laughing. To begin with I didn't realise how important that was. Then I realised I really hadn't laughed properly about little things like that for so long.
Like for example I get annoyed about his smoking, and he tries so hard to stop me being able to smell the smoke. He smokes on the balcony or outside the building.
But however much he tries, the smell is still there on his clothes or his hands, and I don't like it.
His smoking even makes him snore and wake me up at night.
And I always nag him and tell him to stop smoking, and he always puts up with my nagging.
Until one day he told me a really nice story.
He said: I always used to smell my dad's smoke.
It smelled nice and completely different to the smoke outside the house.
The smell itself was linked to a sound.
This one.

MUHAMMAD *rubs the palms of his hands together, making a gentle sound.*

That's how Dad would crumble his tobacco and mix in hashish.
It was the hashish that made the smell of Dad's cigarettes different to the ones I smelled outside.
But I didn't know that at the time.
I used to think it was a special smell that came from my dad himself.
From him. Maybe his saliva. But definitely from Dad's body. A smell that mixed with the smoke he was breathing in and then came out with the smell of the hash.

Dad used to smoke in his bedroom.
The bedroom opened out onto the balcony.
And on the balcony I used to play and I used to smell.

And when I found out that the special smell was just the smell of hash … I was shocked.
Genuinely shocked. That my dad smoked hash!

I went and told a friend of mine in the neighborhood. I said: You won't believe it—turns out my dad smokes hash!
And my friend said: What, didn't you know?
I said: No, I didn't know. I'm shocked.
And he said: By the way, your dad doesn't just smoke hash. Your dad fucks your mum too!

I said: No, that's impossible, what are you talking about? There's no way my dad fucks my mum! My dad fucks *your* mum!!
I wanted to hit him, but my friend got me to understand what he was saying, and explained it was normal for my dad to fuck my mum!!
So I got two shocks about my dad in one day.
The day I found out he smoked hash, I found out he fucked my mum too.

And now, Aline?
How should we go on?

ALINE
No idea.

MUHAMMAD
I liked it! It's really good.
I liked how you moved from one place to the next.
I liked how he slowly got into your life. How he lived at yours and how he gradually took control of everything there, so quietly and nicely. And the thing I liked most was how you implicitly agreed to it, and it was like you were making his task easier for him.
I liked how the relationship slowly seeps into you and everything that happens in it is happening out of love.

But it feels like you're using me a lot?
When I read what you've written, I feel like I'm looking in a mirror!

ALINE
I want to feel like I'm really close to him. Like I love him.

MUHAMMAD
He even has my name.

ALINE
And when I think of him, I see your face.

MUHAMMAD
And now, what do you want to do now?

ALINE
Nothing. Just behave normally.

MUHAMMAD
I wasn't talking about myself. What's it got to do with me? I was talking about the writing. What's going to happen next?

ALINE
No idea. I'll keep on writing to the end.

MUHAMMAD
And him?

ALINE
What about him?

MUHAMMAD
How will he develop? Where do you think you're going to take him in what you're writing?

ALINE
Nowhere.

MUHAMMAD
You have a character who's a former member of the secret police living in your house, and having a relationship with you, and watching you write about your story with a former member of the secret police like him, and you're copying your relationship with him in your writing, and you want him to stay passive like that, not saying anything or doing anything?

ALINE
I'm not copying my relationship with him, I'm copying my relationship with you!

MUHAMMAD
Yes but I mean the whole time we're hearing your voice and finding out about your thoughts and feelings, and we're not finding anything out about him. We know what you're saying and how you're seeing him, but he's not getting any space at all.

ALINE
I understand what you're saying and I did actually think about that.
I tried to write something like what you're suggesting but I really couldn't find a way to do it.
I have the feeling he's going to stay silent, observing things, and not doing anything.
By chance he managed to get into my life and observe it from the inside.
He managed to live with me and sleep with me, but he can't go any further than that. That's the limit of what he can do.

His feelings? What do you mean—that he might feel regret, or something?
Yes, maybe. But what does it matter to me if he regrets what he did or not?
Why would I want to give him the space for us to hear his feelings and his thoughts? Or sit and write and come up with things so that we can understand his psychological make-up and how he became a member of the secret police and how he suddenly started feeling stuck and wanted to leave but couldn't, and how he slipped further into violence against the detainees! No, why would I bother with any of that? How could that be of any interest to someone reading it today?
If one day he's caught and put on trial, he can say all that stuff to his lawyer. His emotional journey and his feelings and his complex motives and I don't know what else. That's useful for him in court, but here in my writing what use is it for us?

MUHAMMAD
But why do you assume he regrets it?
It might be the opposite.
Remember that at the end of the day he's a member of the secret police.

Maybe he wants to hurt you.
Honestly everything you're talking about could be nothing compared to what he's really feeling inside himself.
I can assure you.
You're talking about a guy who probably wants to hurt you.
Kill you, maybe.
Or at least control you.
Maybe when he found out you had been detained, it brought back all his old violence.
You're an example of the sort of person who's always trying to wipe him off the face of the earth.
Imagine ... One meter away from him and there's nothing he can do.
Think of the pressure he's feeling.
Everything he escaped from has come back to life right in front of him.
He tried hard to control his violent thoughts towards you, and he succeeded.
He succeeded to a large extent. At least until now!
But he didn't have many options.
Either he hurts you and kills you and then he gets into big trouble—it's effectively suicide.
Or he runs away, leaves this town and disappears from your life. But he doesn't want to run away again.
Or the final option that's left is loving you.
And the more he loves you, the greater his desire to control you.
It's a big vicious circle and he doesn't know where it'll take him.
There's this massive struggle going on inside him and it doesn't have any impact on you.

ALINE
What you're saying is nice, but to be honest it doesn't matter to me.
I want to judge him in silence!

MUHAMMAD
Even if he's thinking about killing you!

ALINE
Why?

Answer that and I'll be ready to work on it.
Why would he want to kill me or hurt me or control me?
Isn't the terror I've lived through enough?
The interrogation, the insults, the beatings, the torture, the prison cells—in groups and solitary—don't you think that's enough for him to feel like he's won?
I mean in practice he has killed me.

And in the writing, he's seeing with his own eyes how in practice he killed me.
Why don't you read the text like that?!

What's the difference?
He can relax.
He can be proud of himself.
And I even got out of the station alive, with nothing wrong with me.
I can tell you that a part of me died and can't come back to life again.
The part of me that stayed alive will never be well and will never let me be happy.
Even if I could escape and make it here, what does all that mean?
I'm not happy and I don't even feel safe.
Rest assured.
I will live the rest of my life with the shock and the fear and the depression and the guilt.
And even if I tried to write what I lived through, I won't be able to.
I'll always be stuck in a spiral of mirrors.

He can die happy and proud of himself.
He managed to kill me a thousand times, so why would he insist on killing me with his hands as well?

Why would he insist on controlling me and not letting me go?
I know I'm limiting him.
I know I'm writing about him without analyzing his character or assessing his motives and considering them from different perspectives and bringing out the humanity in them.
I do.
I'm not going to be able to present him as a human.

Outside my writing he's a criminal, and inside my writing he's also no more than a criminal.

MUHAMMAD

What you said just now is really good. I wish you could put it in your writing.
Add the new pages to the old ones and send it off.

ALINE

No, not yet.
I've still got a few days and I need to write more.

MUHAMMAD

It's good as it is. Don't write more.

ALINE

No, no. A bit more.

MUHAMMAD

Come on, Aline, it's enough.

Short silence.

Aline, I've got to go.
I've got to get out of here a bit.
I'm going away for a few days.
A week or two.
Not sure where yet.
I want to get a bit of distance.
I need it.

ALINE

Now?
You can't stay till it's finished?

MUHAMMAD

Let me get away.
It'll be better.
I'm exhausted and need some space.
If you think about it for a moment, you'll see it's a very normal thing

to ask.
It's normal for people to go on holiday for a few days to a place they don't know and then come back again.
People are always doing that.
We haven't known each other for long anyway.

ALINE
I won't be able to carry on without you.

MUHAMMAD
You've already written enough.
You just need to send a sample. That's what you said.
Add what you just said to what you've already written and send it off.
I think the length you've written is good.

ALINE
No it's not good.
The length has nothing to do with what I'm writing.
If I send the bit I've written up till now, it won't be clear what I'm doing. And I definitely won't get the grant.

If you leave me like this now, I'll hit a wall and I won't be able to write any more.
I'll collapse. I'll get ill. And when the deadline comes I won't send it.
And if I don't send it I'll go into a new spiral of shit.
I'm only asking you for one thing. I'm begging you.

Stay here. Let us finish the writing and then go wherever you want.
Let's make a proper plan.
Let's hunker down and sign up to a set of rules so we can be sure we'll get the writing done on time.
Rules, yes. Strict rules.
No going out, no visits.
A daily schedule for getting up and eating and work and exercise and rest.
You can even take my mobile. You can keep it. And I'll be allowed to look at it at specific times.

We won't talk about anything else.

If there's something we absolutely have to talk about then we'll do it in a few short sentences.
And every day at an agreed time you'll come in and read what I've written.

If you like it and you don't have many comments you'll be nice to me.
You'll talk to me more or make me a nice hot meal or maybe let me look at my mobile for a bit longer.
And if you don't like the work, it'll be the opposite.
You'll be the opposite of how you normally are and you won't care about me. You'll bring me a small, cold meal and you'll ignore any complaints.

Just when the writing is nearly done, you disappear.
When the end is just a few pages away, you're not here any more.
You throw me out of the way and leave and shut the door in my face.

Silence.

MUHAMMAD
You're right, actually.
It's not important for us to know anything about his interior world.
What's important is for us to focus on you—only you.
But even on that, I can see there's still work to do.

ALINE
I don't understand.

MUHAMMAD
I mean there's still a lot of work you could be doing on that element, to make it clearer.

ALINE
Like what, for example?

MUHAMMAD
There are lots of examples.

ALINE
Like?

MUHAMMAD

Like I remember the first day I saw you, you were introducing yourself to the students in the class and you spoke about your experience of being arrested.

During class you took every opportunity to explain where you came from. Sometimes you were desperate to show them how it was such a closed country and how it was so full of violence and discrimination and corruption and ignorance. And other times you got annoyed when they said anything negative, and you explained to everyone how we're civilized and liberated too and how not everyone has to wear the hijab, and how we have people who drink alcohol and how there are mixed marriages.

I used to see you doing all of this.

I mean there was all this pressure that was falling on you and only you could feel.

It really crushed you that the whole world was just getting on with life and didn't know anything about your tragedies.

I really do know how unpleasant that feeling is.

I used to see how you were desperate to make sure people didn't stop being interested in you and the country.

It was so easy for them to hear what you were saying and be affected by it, and then for it all to quickly disappear and everything to go back to normal.

I saw how that affected you.

I felt for you when you started arriving late so that everyone would see you and remember you were there.

I saw how sometimes when something funny happened you would laugh louder than the others, or longer.

I saw how once when none of this was working, you got up in the middle of class and took your stuff and walked out.

That really was striking. I remember everyone went quiet for a few seconds after you closed the door behind you before the teacher carried on with the class.

Most of the students were foreigners. They came here to do a Masters or a PhD or they worked here as engineers or doctors or researchers, and they came to the language class in the evening after a long and

tiring day. And some of them were foreigners who had married a local and had to learn the language.
And there was a time when you missed a few classes in a row and when you came back you were expecting the students to ask you straight away about why you'd been away. And when no one asked you were disappointed.

In the last part of the course, you were totally silent. You didn't talk about anything or share any opinions.
Always quiet and sitting at the back so no one could see you or remember you were there.
You only answered when the teacher asked you.
Apart from that—absolutely nothing.
Even then your silence was a protest.
But as you know, what happened is everything just carried on as normal.
Days went by. There weren't so many classes. The course was coming to an end.

Why don't you write about all of that?
Why don't you work on it?
Why don't you write about how upset you were?
Why don't you write about how it was so difficult for you to have to do a normal language course?
Just a language course three times a week, two hours each lesson, 120 hours in total.
How impossible it was for you to do 120 hours spread over four months without breaking down.
How difficult it was for you to believe that those 120 hours were just an amount of time to learn a language.
You had to see it as a battlefield on which you could show a few foreign students what your country was and what was happening inside it now and what was happening inside you.

That's just an example that occurred to me now when we were talking.
Just one example of the way you behaved in one part of your life here.
Just one simple, limited example, but it shows us clearly how badly damaged you are.

If you don't like that one I can suggest lots of others.
When we meet someone from the west, how you behave like you're inferior.
When we meet someone from home, how you start being hostile for no reason.
When you drink a lot, how you start talking and crying.
When you dream you've gone back home and you see how repressed you are.
When you totally break down because of some small thing to do with language or when someone talks to you or even looks at you in a way you don't like.
Your endless fantasies about the town blowing up and killing everyone, or about someone dying under a train.

Short silence.

ALINE
And what were you thinking when you were looking at me while I was doing all this?

MUHAMMAD
When exactly?
I gave a lot of examples.

ALINE
In the language course.
What were you thinking when you were looking at me while I was doing everything you described?

MUHAMMAD
You want the truth?

ALINE
Yes, I want it.

MUHAMMAD
Through the whole lot I was only thinking about one thing.
Just how I wanted to sleep with you.
That's the only thought that was in my mind the whole way through

the course.
I didn't see any of what I told you. I mean I saw it but I didn't pay any attention. I wasn't concentrating. My attention was only on one thing.
You!
And to be more precise, my attention on you was focused on only one thing.
Your ass!
You could say your ass was the main reason for my excellent attendance record—I didn't miss a single one.
At the start of the course I kept on thinking I should speak to you.
But when I saw how mad you were I was scared and backed away.
I used to tell myself if I made one wrong move I could be stuck with you in some never-ending story.
For a few moments of happiness I could pay a very high price. Because it was clear that getting stuck with you wouldn't be easy at all.
So I checked myself.
I said: Come on, mate, look after yourself. That girl looks like she's wrong in the head.
And your ass was my companion for that whole time.
Its image stayed with me wherever I went.
For me your ass was like a moving legend!
The legend!

Short silence.

ALINE
Okay then. As you like.

MUHAMMAD
What do you mean, as I like?

ALINE
Go. Don't you want to go?

MUHAMMAD
Thanks.

ALINE
Why are you still here?

MUHAMMAD
I didn't mean right now!

ALINE
Then when?

MUHAMMAD
When I've worked out where I want to go.

ALINE
Get out of here now and then work out where you want to go. And then go where you want to go.

MUHAMMAD
I don't understand you, Aline.

ALINE
What don't you understand about "get out of here now"?!

MUHAMMAD
Are you serious?

ALINE
Yes.

MUHAMMAD
What's going on? What's happened to you?
You want to chuck me out because I want to take a few days holiday? Okay, fine. With pleasure. Tomorrow morning when you wake up I'll be gone.

ALINE
Why tomorrow morning? Your place isn't far away.

MUHAMMAD
Oh that's how it is now!
Okay.

He picks up some of his things and starts to leave.

And are you going to use what just happened in your writing too?

ALINE
Yes.

MUHAMMAD
What are you going to say? That you got the better of a member of the secret police by throwing him out of your house at midnight?
What sort of achievement is that? What sort of wonderful writing?
And why did it happen? Because he asked if he could take a few days off on his own!
How profound!
Let me congratulate you!

ALINE
No, it's not him I'm going to deal with like that. This is just for you.

MUHAMMAD
Ah. I understand!
Fine, how about I don't leave!

ALINE
No, no—you're going to leave.

MUHAMMAD
No. I'm not leaving.
I'll sit down here for as long as I like!

ALINE
Muhammad, it's not a joke. Please leave like I asked you to.

MUHAMMAD
I'll leave when I want.
Do you understand?
I'm not the sort of person who can be told when to leave and when to come in.

ACT THREE

MUHAMMAD *is reading.*

ALINE *is standing on the balcony, holding a bunch of keys.*

MUHAMMAD
Act Three.
I was expecting him to stay the night and then actually leave in the morning.
That he'd stay the night here just to annoy me and that would be it.
But what happened was he stayed. He didn't leave the next day.
Time went on, the morning ended, then the afternoon and then it was evening and he still hadn't left.
He hadn't even packed his bag or given any sign that he was going to leave soon.
Absolutely nothing. Everything he was doing suggested he was staying. Who knows till when.
We didn't say a word to each other.
After our argument I didn't say anything and ignored him. He did the same.
This ignoring each other started that night and lasted for days.
It's hard to say how much time passed.
I was expecting any moment I would turn round and he would be gone.
He wanted to make me angry. That's all. So I let him and told myself he'd get bored. A day or two and he'd get tired of it and go off on his own.
I tried to focus on myself and totally ignore him. That meant I stopped really knowing what he was doing.
If he was in the kitchen, I'd go to the sitting room. If he came to the sitting room, I'd lock myself away in my room. And if he went out to smoke on the balcony, I'd go to the kitchen.

Sometimes I'd be eating and look up and see him sitting in front of me.

And sometimes I'd watch him standing on the balcony or sitting on the sofa or even having a shower.
I started seeing him a lot in my dreams.
And when I opened my eyes in the night, I'd see him lying next to me.

As time went by, we learnt how to avoid each other and not come face to face.
I really stopped seeing him very much at all but I could still see his traces about the place.
When I went into the kitchen to make food, everything would be dirty.
The sink was filled with dirty plates and pans.
The bin was overflowing.
Beer and wine bottles all over the place.
Mess everywhere.
Everything was broken.
Nothing was where it should be or where I'd left it.
Sometimes he'd leave the TV or the radio on and go away.

However awful it was, on some level inside me I was enjoying seeing how low a human could go.

But in reality I was suffocating.
At a certain point I couldn't bear it anymore.

I had to speak to him and ask him to leave.
I left him a short note on the table.
"I beg you to get out of my life."
He saw the piece of paper and read the note and didn't react.
Everything stayed as it was.

The next morning I woke up really choking.
If he stayed in my life for another minute I'd either kill him or kill myself.
I came out of my room wanting to give him hell if he didn't disappear from my life that day.
But he wasn't there. I looked for him everywhere in the house and he wasn't there.

He was really gone!
His things were still there—just a few bits of clothes.
Could he really have just got up and gone?
Maybe he'll come back to get them later?
I wasn't going to wait. I packed all his things into a bag and decided to leave them at the door to his house.
Time went by and no one came.
At the end of the day, I was going to be on my own for the first time in weeks.
I've got to sort everything and give the place a proper clean, but I can do that tomorrow.
I celebrated!
I opened a bottle of wine and turned on some music and relaxed.

After a few glasses I was flying.
I went to bed early and fell straight asleep.
I was woken up suddenly by a noise in the night.
The noise was clear and there was no other explanation for it.
A man and a woman having sex.
The noise was coming from the sitting room.
I could hear him.
It was him.
Motherfucker bringing a girl back to my house!
I was going to go and scream at them but I got scared.
I felt scared and embarrassed.
I froze where I was.
Their voices were loud—like they wanted me to hear.
I buried my head under my pillow and the blanket and I screwed my eyes shut and curled up my body.
I started crying and shaking and got louder and louder.

I woke up in the morning and got dressed and went out of the house without looking around me at all.
I went through the sitting room but I really didn't let myself look around or see if they were still there or not.
I slammed the door behind me and went down the stairs.

I left the building and turned left and then right.
After ten minutes I was there.
I went up to the floor where the investigations department was and went inside.
The man behind the desk asked me if I had an appointment and what I was there for.
I said I didn't have an appointment and I was there to report on someone who had been involved in the torture and murder of people inside a security agency before he left the country and came here about a year ago to claim asylum.
The man asked me to say what I'd told him again. When I repeated it, he asked me to wait to the side for a bit. He picked up his phone and called someone and asked them to come.
A woman came and it was clear she was somehow important.
She introduced herself to me and asked me to repeat what I'd said, and then she asked me to come with her.
We went into an office and she started asking me questions to get me to tell her what I'd come to say again, but this time in detail.
Detail!
And what details!
His first name, his surname, with the possibility that he had changed his name, naturally.
His address and phone number. He had sent me his address in a message with the code for the door too.
His appearance. I showed them a clear picture of his face that I took one time without him noticing. He absolutely refused to be photographed, as it happens!
My relationship with him. I met him at a language course and now he's my friend.
Friend, what do I mean by friend? Boyfriend, if you'd prefer.
Still?
Yes, still!
Evidence. Is there any evidence in support of your claims?
Of course.
Me.
I am the evidence.

Me and my fantasies!!
What are they?
Mainly post-traumatic stress disorder, as well as addictive behaviour and suicidal thoughts. In addition, obsessive compulsive disorder, depression, and generalized anxiety.
Do you take any psychiatric medications regularly?
Of course. Regularly and irregularly.
Do you take any drugs likes hashish?
Absolutely.
Alcohol?
Naturally.
I know what I am saying isn't logical and I know everything I'm claiming could just be an illusion, but I'm begging you to give me a chance. Give my pathological fantasies one chance. What do you have to lose? If it turns out they're true then you'll have caught a criminal who escaped from justice, and if they turn out to be wrong then you'll have found a sick person who decided not to live in silence with her fantasies. That's interesting too!
She thanked me kindly, apologized to me and walked me to the door.

At the door, before I went, I wanted to tell her that I'd written everything that happened now on some paper and left it on the table in the flat and Muhammad would probably be sitting reading it now. Muhammad would probably know I was in a police station filing a report against him and accusing him of being a criminal. But I got scared. I didn't say anything. I said goodbye like an idiot and walked off. I was too scared to say anything. Fear got the better of me. Maybe if she'd been a bit nicer to me, I would have had the courage to speak. But she was very formal with me.

As usual, I'm blaming others. If she'd been a tiny bit nicer I would have had the courage to tell her that my life was in danger after coming to the police because I actually told the criminal that I was going to report on him—that I was now reporting on him!

On my way home, I went to the supermarket. I spent everything I had on food. Everything you can think of. I filled a big trolley.

When I got home I saw exactly what I was expecting.
Muhammad was awake and reading.
When I came in he looked at me and the hundred bags I was carrying.
He watched how I put everything on the floor. How I got out the keys and locked the door from the inside and how I quietly walked onto the balcony. The place I only very rarely went. How I lifted up the keys and held my hand out over the edge and looked at how they were swinging before ...

ALINE *opens her fingers and the keys fall down.*

I watched how they fell from the ninth floor and how you could hear the noise they made as they hit the ground.
At that moment Abu Hamid stopped reading.

MUHAMMAD *stops reading, and says the next section addressing* ALINE.

He stops and he walks towards me. He goes out onto the balcony and stands next to me. Right next to me.

He and I look at each other at the same time. We look down to where the keys fell and then we look at each other again, then ahead. Each of us is staring ahead at some point in space.

A long time passes. Properly long. A few minutes.
And finally Muhammad undoes his trousers and takes his dick out and pisses over the edge.
He takes a long piss from the balcony on the ninth floor.

The sight of his piss falling down is an unforgettable sight!
The more distance it covered on its way down, the more the droplets separated from each other and spread out.
A gentle breeze pushed it slightly to the right, making the scene a little more realistic.
The final thing I want to say in this epic piece of theatre—please listen carefully—is that there was one main stream of Muhammad's piss that I've described to you, and there were some much smaller

drops that were flying to the right and the left in the breeze. Tiny little specks of drizzle.
They completed the scene.

That's all I wanted to add!

Thank you.

The End.

Silence.

Why did you do that?

ALINE
Because you're a motherfucker.

MUHAMMAD
I'm not asking why you reported on me.
My question is why did you come back here?
Do you want to kill yourself or what?
Can you imagine how much danger you've put yourself in?
Can you imagine what I could do to you now?
Why are you locking yourself in with someone who has a hundred reasons to hurt you?
I mean—who would blame me for anything violent I did to you now?
What do you want?
Do you want straight up physical violence? You want me to hit you and gag you and tie you up and beat you or something?
Or do you want different types of violence? Like spitting in your food before you eat it? Or stopping you from sleeping by shining lights and making noise? Or pissing all over the place like you suggested in your wonderful scene? Aline, you really can't imagine the things I can do to drive you properly mad.
Then you'll actually throw yourself off this balcony to end it all!
What?
You don't want to carry on living?
You're done? You want to end it here?
You want to die with the past?

Anyway, even the way it ends in what you've written is no good.
You coming back here and locking us up with each other inside the flat and inside the story and leaving the ending open like that—trust me you've got it wrong! There's no way that's how it should be.
The only good thing in it is that you've grasped the problem you're writing about.
You've grasped it and you're making us understand, through the symbolism of locking the door and throwing away the key, that you've grasped it.
Finally you've understood that the problem is that your world is closing in, or your relationship with your surroundings and with the past is disappearing.
But you got it wrong, Aline, when you came back here. You got it even more wrong when you locked yourself in with me.
Did you want to give people a bit of hope?
Can you imagine what will happen to anyone who reads your writing?
They'll get depressed!
People won't like it like this.
But of course you aren't going to submit the file for the grant, and you're not going to publish it, because I'm probably going to kill you.
I say probably because there's still a chance that you'll get on with your life and get on with your writing.
Get out of here, Aline.
It'd be better for both of us, trust me.
Take this last chance and try to sort out what you've done.
Let's both get out of this story alive.

Silence.

ALINE
Help me.

MUHAMMAD
What did you say?

ALINE
I said help me. I can't come up with anything anymore.

MUHAMMAD
I don't know.
Get well away from where you've ended up.
Get back to the moment you left the police station and stood in the street not knowing what to do.
Start from there.
Stand in the street and think about it properly.
Work out exactly what you want and how you're going to get there.
What did you actually want to achieve from going to the police station?

ALINE
Them to catch you.

MUHAMMAD
And why didn't that happen?

ALINE
I didn't have any evidence.

MUHAMMAD
You see? Now we're getting somewhere. All it takes is one logical question and you can find your story.

ALINE
Okay, but where can I get evidence from?

MUHAMMAD
Where?

ALINE
You're not going to come clean.

MUHAMMAD
I'm definitely not going to give you any evidence.
So, what then?
Where could you find some evidence against me?

ALINE
Your flat.
If you've left evidence anywhere, it'll be in your flat.

MUHAMMAD
Very sensible.

ALINE
Your flat that I've only been into once.

MUHAMMAD
Right.

ALINE
After the police I'm going to come up with the idea of going to your flat to look for the evidence I need.
But I haven't got a key.

MUHAMMAD
Don't worry about that. Change the order of events. Let's say you had the idea in mind from the start. From before you left here.
Let's make you a bit cleverer and say you decided from the start that your objective was to do me in.
You had the idea of the flat and the evidence and the search from the beginning. That makes more sense anyway actually.
You'll take my key from here. And you'll go to the flat first.
You'll go in and painstakingly search the flat, making sure you leave everything exactly where it was, because you're afraid of what you're doing.
You don't find anything so you get on with the main part of the plan—reporting me to the police.
You go to the police station and you don't get anywhere because you don't have any evidence.
Then you go back to my flat and you turn the place upside down. You don't have anything to lose now. If you don't find anything that proves I'm guilty then it's all over anyway. You won't leave the flat until you've found something that helps you.

ALINE
Will I find anything?

MUHAMMAD

I don't know. I'm just bringing some options for your story and trying to create a chance—even a small one—of us staying alive.
If I'm secret police and I've left some evidence you'll find it and hand me in to the police. If you don't find anything then I'm either innocent or I'm very smart and haven't left a trace of anything. In either case, I deserve to live.
Here's the key to my flat.
Now call someone who can bring your keys from down there.
And as soon as the door's open, get out of here.

Silence.

ALINE

After I've searched the flat and not found anything I'm going to be really tired.
I'll take a break. I'll make some food. Then maybe I'll have a lie down.
And when I fall asleep it'll be the first time for ages that I don't dream of him.
The only place where his shadow disappears is in your flat.
That's the evidence against you that I'll get.
I know that sort of evidence isn't worth anything in court but it's enough for me and that's what matters most.
It's enough for me—just me—to be sure that my shitty luck got me mixed up with a criminal on the run who took my flat and whose flat I took in return.
I'll stay there.
I'll live there.
Your home will become my home.
I imagine I'll be comfortable in your flat.
Not too high up and no balcony.
Your mirrors will show my face.
Your sofa is where I rest.
Your neighbors will be mine.
Your flat is the first thing I see in the morning.
Maybe we can have an agreement.
A truce.

Each of us pays their bills and checks their post.
Time will pass.
Is there anything stranger than that?!
It will be clear that the story's over.
No winner, no loser.
Totally absurd!
We wait.
I don't know what we're waiting for.
Maybe we wait to meet again.
By chance in the street.
Honestly I don't know what sort of place could bring us together again.
It would have to be a new language course.
Makes sense.
I actually don't know what we'd say to each other.
Can you imagine?
There.
By the coffee machine.
By the coffee machine at the break.
We'll meet.

Short silence.

Muhammad I know you're secret police. I don't need any evidence.
And I know that the more I accuse you, the clearer it'll be that you're innocent and I'm mad.
But that's actually not the point.
I mean even if you really are innocent, I'll keep on accusing you.
If one day I get back to being normal, that's when you'll be innocent!
The issue I have isn't an issue of having to get justice.
Fuck justice.
The issue I have is much simpler than that.
Instead of losing my life in silence, I decided to lose it loudly.
That's all it is.

PART ONE OF THE FINAL ACT

ALINE
Does your coffee have any sugar in it?

MUHAMMAD
Yes.

ALINE
Did you ask for it with sugar or did you press for no sugar and it came out with?

MUHAMMAD
I don't understand.

ALINE
This stupid machine always gives me coffee with sugar when I ask for it without.

MUHAMMAD
Did you set the sugar level right?

ALINE
Yes I did but it went and gave me coffee with sugar anyway.

MUHAMMAD
I get it.

ALINE
I can't drink it. Fills you up with sugar.

Short silence.

MUHAMMAD
Maybe we should go back.

ALINE
Are you trying to avoid me?

MUHAMMAD
A bit.

ALINE
Why?

MUHAMMAD
I'm joking. I'm not trying to avoid you—I'm just like that.
I avoid everyone.

ALINE
Everyone?

MUHAMMAD
Yes everyone. I even avoid myself in a way.
I don't mingle.
You see I can talk a bit to the rest of the students but I only do it for the language.

ALINE
How do you spell your name?

MUHAMMAD
My name?

ALINE
In English, I mean.
I looked for you but I couldn't find you.
I mean on the internet. I wrote your name on Facebook but I couldn't find anything.
People write Muhammad in hundreds of different ways in English. Some people write it Mohamad, with an O and one M. Some people write it Mouhamad, with a U after the O. Some people write it with a double M, so it's Mohammad. And then the best is when people write it Mohammed with an E...

MUHAMMAD
I'm not on Facebook.

ALINE
Yes but how do you write your name in English? The official spelling.

MUHAMMAD
I'll write it out for you but I think we have to go back now.

ALINE
How old are you?
I mean you're not old. There are people who are older than you who have Facebook.

MUHAMMAD
I don't like it.

ALINE
So you had an account and then you deleted it?

MUHAMMAD
No, I've never had one.

ALINE
Ah so you're The Mysterious Man?

MUHAMMAD
What does that mean?

ALINE
In the dark glasses!
The Mysterious Man in the Dark Glasses.
Soad Hosny.
Hey Tough Guy,
I like you and I can wait!

MUHAMMAD
Strange.
I was watching a film about how she died yesterday.

ALINE
What did they say—suicide or murder?

MUHAMMAD
Tending towards murder, killed by the Egyptian secret services.

ALINE
I can only imagine how terrifying those moments before they threw her off must have been.

MUHAMMAD
I really love that film.

ALINE
Watch Out For Zouzou?
I absolutely love it.
I listen to the songs in it all the time.
Salah Jahin.
The poet.
The poet who wrote the script and the song lyrics is the same guy who a few years before was writing songs for the revolution in Egypt, before the Naksa.
It was him who immortalised Gamal Abdel Nasser in his poems.
The President of Egypt and the only Arab leader.

Then they did a film with the same title.
The Mysterious Man.
A comedy.
Don't you know it?
It's very silly.
The star is that beautiful actress who looks like a cat.
Nelly Karim—was that her name?
They used to show it on Melody.
You know Melody, the one with that program "Defying Boredom."
It was them who produced the film too.
The producer's called Gamal Marwan.
A businessman.
A millionaire.
He owned the whole Melody network.
His dad was called Ashraf Marwan. Another businessman, and a politician too.

He really was a very mysterious man.
He was killed in his flat in London in 2007.
He fell from his balcony too and they recorded it as suicide.
The CCTV on the street wasn't working.
That's what the British police said.
They say he was a double agent for Israel and Egypt.
In Egypt he's a hero.
Ashraf's wife was called Mona.
Mona Abdel Nasser.
The daughter of Gamal Abdel Nasser.
You see how it all comes back to the one and only Gamal?
The hero of Arab Nationalism and the nationalization of the Suez Canal.
The one whose life they made a film about called Nasser 56.
With Ahmed Zaki playing Nasser.
May he rest in peace.
Ahmed Zaki was the best Arab actor I've ever seen.
It never felt like he was acting.

MUHAMMAD
There's a film where he plays an honest policeman who goes undercover in the drug business.

ALINE
Land of Fear.

MUHAMMAD
Exactly. *Land of Fear.*
That's my favorite film of his.

ALINE
Yeah I really like it too. But I have to say I didn't have you down as a film fan.

MUHAMMAD
No, I watch a lot of films.
You can find them all on YouTube.
I watch a lot of old ones.
I used to rent them.

But I can't remember the titles and the stories and the names like you can.

ALINE
What was your job?

MUHAMMAD
Oh I was just a taxi driver.

ALINE
Secret police, then.

MUHAMMAD
Exactly.

ALINE
I'm joking. Sorry.

MUHAMMAD
No it's fine.

ALINE
If you were secret police then I wouldn't have met you here, would I?

MUHAMMAD
You never know!

Short silence.

The thing I love most about that film is when he gets to the stage where he can't tell who he is anymore.
When he sleeps with his wife and she doesn't want to.

ALINE
Exactly. That scene is so upsetting. She wants to get away from him after she's found out he's a drug dealer. And he loves her so much and he can't tell her he's working for the police.

Short silence.

Don't you want to go back?

MUHAMMAD
Where? Home?

ALINE
No, to class.

MUHAMMAD
To the class that's about to finish?

PART TWO OF THE FINAL ACT

MUHAMMAD *and* ALINE *are in a bar.*

They are sitting at a high table on bar stools. They each have a glass of wine.

They are talking but we cannot hear what they are saying because loud music is playing.

It is clear that they are enjoying themselves and having an interesting conversation.

The music is lively.

FINAL PART OF THE FINAL ACT

ALINE
And it's like in the films. The co-stars arrive at the leading lady's place at the end of the night.

MUHAMMAD
This is where you live?

ALINE
Yes.

MUHAMMAD
Not far from me. I'm about ten minutes' walk away.

ALINE
Seriously? Great.
They are silent for a moment and don't know what to say.

MUHAMMAD
Exactly.

ALINE
That was fun.

MUHAMMAD
Yes it was.

ALINE
Are you coming to class tomorrow?

MUHAMMAD
There's no class tomorrow.

ALINE
Oh yes. That's right.
It's good, our class.

MUHAMMAD
Yes, it's alright.

ALINE
Are you going to do the next course?

MUHAMMAD
Yes definitely.

ALINE
And suddenly they are silent again.

MUHAMMAD
Yes, they don't know how they should end things.

ALINE
Yes, they are a bit embarrassed.

MUHAMMAD
Exactly. Well, how many floors does this building have?

ALINE
Good effort. This building has nine floors.

MUHAMMAD
And which floor are you on?

ALINE
The top floor.

MUHAMMAD
Wow. That's high.

ALINE
Do you have agoraphobia?

MUHAMMAD
You mean vertigo?

ALINE
Bravo!

MUHAMMAD
No. I'm just drawing the conversation out a bit.

Do you have a balcony?

ALINE
Yes.

MUHAMMAD
Lucky you. I don't and I'd really like to live somewhere with a balcony.

ALINE
We'll have to swap then.
I've got really bad vertigo. I barely ever go out on the balcony!

MUHAMMAD
A cruel twist of fate!

ALINE
An awkward silence prevails. Muhammad and Aline do not want to stop here.

MUHAMMAD
I'd like a balcony just so I could smoke.
You know that's one of the things that makes me regret having come here?
Seriously. I'm not joking.
Not being able to smoke where I want to.
There's always something to ruin my mood.
Whenever I want to smoke I have to open the window or go out onto the street.
Smoking's not allowed in my flat. There's an alarm.
I tried to turn it off once. I didn't know what I was doing and I set it off.
It started mooing like a cow. Two minutes later security were at the door.
I was scared of trying again and I don't know anyone in this shitty town who would help me to turn the thing off.
It's so sensitive. It went off once when I was cooking.
It took me an hour to convince security I hadn't been smoking.
They gave me a warning!
Since then I haven't even tried smoking out of the window.

I go downstairs, die from the cold, and go back up.
I don't like smoking standing up or walking anyway.
Anywhere you go smoking's not allowed.
I don't have anyone I see or talk to apart from Amer, when he comes to visit every now and again.
So cigarettes really are my way of having fun.
I don't want to see anyone anyway. I want to be on my own.
The height of my ambitions is to sit on my sofa and smoke and drink and let my mind go.
What's happened to the old days?
The days when we could smoke wherever we wanted, whenever we wanted.
Even in planes!
That's all gone now.
Gone and not coming back, sadly.
When I made up my mind and decided to leave, I thought through everything apart from that.
It never occurred to me. Simple as that.
The most important thing in my life and I didn't give it a moment's thought.
If I'd known I'd be so bothered by the smoking, I wouldn't have left.
Trust me.
I'm not joking.
No, I'm not happy here.
Every day I hope I'll die.
I feel like my life here is one long punishment.
And you know all the shit we live with here? I could put up with it all if I could smoke when I feel like it.
Like a person with dignity.

ALINE

Who's Amer?

MUHAMMAD

Amer!

ALINE
You mentioned him just now—you said he comes to visit every now and then.

MUHAMMAD
My son.

ALINE
Okay.

MUHAMMAD
He doesn't live here. He found a job and moved away.

ALINE
Oh that's great.

MUHAMMAD
Computer engineer.

ALINE
Brilliant.

MUHAMMAD
Yes he got his degree transferred and studied for two years and then he got a job.
He used to visit a lot and then his visits got much rarer.
Now he's got his life over there. What's he got to do here now?

ALINE
I've got to go up.

MUHAMMAD
Of course. Goodbye.

ALINE
Goodnight.

MUHAMMAD
That's what happens at the end of the conversation.

ALINE
What do you mean?

MUHAMMAD
When one of the co-stars does something wrong.
He says something he shouldn't have said and… and the moment's gone.

ALINE
What was it that you shouldn't have said?

MUHAMMAD
About Amer.

ALINE
Why do you think that was wrong?

MUHAMMAD
Silence.

ALINE
No there's no need for silence
I got upset with myself, not with you.
I got upset because I've been here for a few years and I still haven't done anything with my life. I am still all over the place.
I am getting benefits and learning the language and getting depressed and getting treatment and getting depressed again.
But I'm not failing that badly!
And I'm going to finish another level of the language classes, and I'm definitely going to pass.
And I'm actually doing something really important that I haven't told anyone about.
I'm writing something.

MUHAMMAD
A story?

ALINE
I don't know.

MUHAMMAD
What's it about?

ALINE
I don't know that either.
Maybe a love story!

MUHAMMAD
Do you want to get it published?

ALINE
I'm submitting it for a publishing grant and the deadline is soon. I'm still working on the précis and I have to write at least one part or one chapter.

ALINE *waits for* MUHAMMAD *to make a comment or any attempt to continue the conversation, but he stays frozen.*

ALINE *decides to put an end to the awkwardness by smiling and heading towards the entrance to the building. Before she closes the door behind her,* MUHAMMAD *speaks.*

MUHAMMAD
I'd like to read it.

ALINE
Did you say something?

MUHAMMAD
I said I'd like to read it.

ALINE
Seriously?

MUHAMMAD
Yes, seriously.
If you like, I can read it and tell you what I think.

ALINE
Of course I'd like that.

MUHAMMAD
How can I get a copy?

ALINE
Email. I'll send you an email.
Write it for me.

ALINE *holds her mobile out to* MUHAMMAD. MUHAMMAD *types his email address into* ALINE*'s phone. At last* ALINE *will know how* MUHAMMAD *writes his name in English! She takes her mobile back from* MUHAMMAD *and tries to read.*

You're joking! What is that? Braveheart75!
I don't believe what I'm seeing! You got that address and you've kept it till now?

MUHAMMAD
At gmail dot com.

ALINE
Yes, I saw that, I saw that.
And 75 is obviously the year you were born.

MUHAMMAD
Yes.

ALINE
You are astonishing.
You'll have it now.

MUHAMMAD
That fast?

ALINE
Yes, that fast. Emails are supposed to arrive immediately.

MUHAMMAD
No I meant—you sent it that fast.

ALINE
Yes I sent it that fast.

MUHAMMAD
I'll read it tonight.

ALINE
Thanks.

MUHAMMAD
Do you want to meet tomorrow?

ALINE
Yes.

MUHAMMAD
In the evening?

ALINE
In the evening.

MUHAMMAD
Where?

ALINE
It doesn't matter.

MUHAMMAD
At mine?

ALINE
At yours.

MUHAMMAD
Okay, I'll send you the address.

ALINE
Okay.

MUHAMMAD
It's not far. Actually ten minutes' walk from here.

ALINE
Great.

MUHAMMAD
I'll send you the code too.

ALINE
Yes, send me the code too.

Short silence.

MUHAMMAD
See you tomorrow.

ALINE
Goodbye, Braveheart.

Yakouta

(Ruby)

by Leila Toubel

translated by Hisham Ben Khamsa

with additional contributions by Haruna Lee

To all who preserve their humanity in a world scarred by monsters.

ON *YAKOUTA*

Across the zoom, I see Leila, a playwright and performer. She sees me, also a playwright and performer. We offer a warm smile to each other but neither of us have spoken a word to each other yet. Next to Leila is Hisham. Hisham is a translator and Leila's close friend and long-time collaborator who has already translated Leila's play *Yakouta* or *Ruby* into English. I was invited into this collaboration to also "translate." But because I don't speak French or Arabic, and the original play was written primarily in Arabic, it was yet to be determined what exactly I'd be translating or how I could make an offering to this process, if at all. As an American theater maker working in both English and Japanese, I wondered about what I could offer. Maybe it was a particular lens or "aesthetic" of multilingual-ness that Leila and I both straddle in our work? Or perhaps the playwright/performer duality that Leila and I share? Or perhaps I could support the experimental nature of this piece through textual design and layout? These ideas only lived on a theoretical plane, though. In reality, we were sitting on a zoom with 4,437 miles between our bodies in Tunis and Brooklyn, and a 6-hour time difference to boot. And despite the abstraction of the invitation that landed us here, the task at hand remained murky. We were all here to support this English version of a Tunisian play and make it more ... make it more ... And if you follow that line of thinking for a little while, I think it opens up a political debate about translation and the hegemony of the English language that starts to stink of American exceptionalism and superiority. And we were all being so very careful not to cross that line.

What I know from my own experience is that spoken language is not the only way to communicate. I knew this from my relationship with my immigrant mom, whose native tongue I am always grasping at. I leaned in when Leila spoke about her work. I could understand her body language perfectly, the practiced way an artist talks about their creative ideas and how those ideas have manifested into performance through duration and dedication, like a snake who knows how to shed its own skin. And when Hisham translated her words, I understood the fiery care and protectiveness he feels for his collaborator, and his love for what she makes. That Leila trusted him with this. I didn't glean these dynamics from what was spoken between us, but from the over-arching language of human feeling and intention, and the approach to art-making that we all feel so strongly about.

I read Hisham's translation of *Yakouta* a number of times before I finally watched a recording of Leila performing it. What felt shadowy and amorphous in the text because of my lack of understanding of Tunisian history and culture suddenly became very clear and intentional: because I understand how to witness and engage with performance. And Leila's performance, it was transcendent. I would watch the video while tracking each beat in the text and then I'd hit pause every time I felt a performative shift—emotional, physical, spatial, structural sometimes conceptual—and I'd write notes to keep track of how this play was moving, in its fractures and as a whole. Once I got through the entire piece this way, I finally had some concrete ideas to share with Leila and Hisham. We worked in tandem, back and forth like this, and what you are about to read is a slightly re-organized structure from the original that we think supports the ephemeral, slippery time-signature of this play, and the terrifying multitude of characters that emerge like never-ending nesting dolls from a single woman who is attempting to voice the strange, absurd, violent, hilarious, and brutally honest voices and opinions about both contemporary and historical femininity and the feminine experience—how we are constantly fighting state, religion, biology, patriarchy and even motherhood in order not to be consumed. And how the way out of our own consumption is only through rage. So naturally, this is a rage play. A poetic rallying cry for all of us who are both mother and child, sacred and feminine.

This play asks a scary question: what survives after the turmoil, after everything that is sacred and feminine is obliterated? The message I receive from Leila's words is: the power and gift of mothering ourselves.

— Haruna Lee

This play is performed by one performer.

A WOMAN *enters a room.*

WOMAN

I have a very cute daughter.

She speaks a lullaby.

Open the door
Open the door
And let me tell you a story
I have a very cute daughter

The Kahia[1] *asked for her hand*
But I don't want to
I won't give her away
I won't give her away
Even for all of Tunisia, I won't give her away

Grace and luck
Grace and luck
Suitors are jostling for her
My daughter has grown up but I won't give her away

I left her when she was just a little thing
Today I will see her again after 24 years.
Longer than eternity.
I got dressed, dolled up and prepped myself
My body was shaking with joy
And my eyes were filled with tears.
I was about to leave,
When I came face to face with my husband.
I don't know how he found out.

He immediately started beating me, foaming and drooling at the lips

HUSBAND

A daughter? You have a daughter?
How? When? Where did she come from?

1 Dignitary

Who is her father?
So you have been cheating on me?
You assured me that you were infertile.
Speak, how did you have her?

SHHHH.

Answer me in silence.
Dirty whore
I saved you.
If it wasn't for me,
You would still be hanging around restaurants and cabarets
Hunting for someone who'd buy you dinner
And put you in his bed afterwards
And at the end of the evening, he'd throw you a few coins.

You were out at dawn
Haggard
Wandering aimlessly.

Until you crossed my path.

You confessed your mistake to me
I saved you
I trampled my honor and my manhood to finally marry you.
Even more,
I spoiled you during our three day honeymoon in a 2-star hotel
So you would feel like a real woman among your peers

I gave you my name
And that's no small thing!
You are now 'Madam'
The wife of your master, the man that I am
A name registered on your national identity card,
On your police record
When a cop stops you and they see that you are married,
The cop respects you
A name that gives you value, respect among people

And elegance on your tomb stone.

A bastard girl?!

I will kill you slowly.
I'll leave you dying of hunger and thirst.
You will die suffocated by the stench of your decline,
Your scandal and your stupidity.
You will rot alone until the worms devour your flesh.
The air will fill with the smell of your carrion body.
Gouging out your eyes won't even be enough for me.
UNFAITHFUL!

And he threw me in a room
And locked me in where I spent half of my life.
This is the room he throws me in every time he beats me
Where he locks me up between four walls
Alone with my aching head, my memories and my story
With my dummy mannequin named Ommek Tfila[2]
Who was offered to me by my neighbor
A deranged artist who hung herself.

She speaks to her HUSBAND.

Open this door,
I will tell you.
You know I'm claustrophobic.
Why don't you talk anymore? Why this silence?
Come hit me, yell and spit in my face.
I'm afraid of the sound of silence, the color of darkness.

A SHIFT. She is returning to a memory from her childhood.

That day my mother locked me in a room
And turned off the light leaving me in total darkness—

2 A character in popular Tunisian culture who is portrayed as an Auntie figure in the form of a clay doll. An enabler of misogyny, Ommek Tfila will listen to your miserable stories and turn them into worms.

This was after I told her that my older brother kissed me on the mouth
Buried his head under my dress and gave me a little booboo—
She tied me to a chair with the belt of her house robe
She cut my long hair with her sewing scissors while babbling

MOTHER
SHHHH ... You will shut your mouth
I will rip your lips off and go so far as to kill you
If you say a single word, utter a single letter.
He kissed you on the mouth because he loves you
And hid his head under your dress to play hide-and-seek with you

With a hot chili pepper she rubbed my lips.

MOTHER
Here is your booboo
Here is your booboo

I felt a hot liquid flow between my thighs ...
I did not move nor resist.
Only my silent tears looking at her
I don't know if I remained tied up for an hour or all night
At first, I was scared
Very scared, but then I closed my eyes ...
I dreamt of myself running after a butterfly in a huge garden
My long hair that my mother had just cut floated in the wind
I parted my long locks to see the butterfly—
That's when I saw him:
My older brother
Standing
Smiling
Smoking a cigarette and blowing the smoke in my face.
When he finished his cigarette he crushed the glowing butt on my thigh
I did not move, I did not resist.
I pursed my lips without shouting
The tears he was expecting did not fall from my glaring eyes

She speaks to her HUSBAND *once again.*

Come on, open that door
And come look me in the eye!
Strike again and continue to bruise the last crevices of my body
And listen to my story.

A SHIFT. Time passes in her memory. She is now a little older.

The wind has swept away the last memory of another night
When the sperm attacked the egg.
I was only 16 years old
I was proud of my youth
In the winter I studied and in the summer I worked as a store clerk
In a small shop to earn my pocket money.
The owner called it a boutique
But it was a cozy shop that sold all sorts of things:
Panties
And blankets with the image of a tiger laying fully stretched
With its mouth open, ready to pounce on its prey
And lipstick.
My boss was very superstitious.
At the store opening she would order me to wash the floors
Play a tape of Quran and perfume the room with incense
But the smell of incense suffocates and sickens me.
And now every day a curvy beautiful woman
Comes to the store to buy something,
Now she's asking about my name
She's asking about my age and my salary
And now she is giving me a banknote to buy some pantyhose
Pressing on my hand, telling me

CURVY BEAUTIFUL WOMAN
Keep the change and get yourself what you want.

When I'm going home in the evening, she's waiting for me in her car
Insisting on giving me a ride.
And one day while lifting my hair
She strokes the back of my neck with her long, red fingernails, telling me

CURVY BEAUTIFUL WOMAN
Beauty, youth and finesse should not be wasted
You should wear the best clothes
Go to hair salons and patronize beauticians
Travel and live in luxury hotels
Have a car with a driver at your disposal
You should sparkle with gold and diamonds.
Come take a break at my house,
I am throwing a party for "High Society."
Indeed, they were from "The High" and way beyond.

I remained frozen
Without eating or speaking.
I watched the women laugh out loud
Their bodies moving to music in full swing
Men poured whiskey into the cleavages
And quenched their thirst in there.
The tapas abounded:
Pistachio, bottarga, cheese, caviar, black and green olives
As for me
I drank a juice with a bitter taste
Served to me by the host of the house …

Time passes. A lapse in consciousness.

I don't know how I found myself
In a room with red sheets and curtains.
The light was dim and red
And a man was lying on the bed next to me
With a crimson face and fiery eyes.

I had a hellish night!

That was the night the egg descended into the uterus.
This man I didn't know—
After a well-wined late-night—
Spewed his seed inside of me.
He looked at my torn clothes, my bare thighs

My tears flowing silently,
And he barked

MAN
The tears of whores turn me on
Be quiet, otherwise my sperm may spurt out

I went back home.
I spent hours washing myself, rubbing myself
To erase his smell
His sweat
His saliva
His voice
His gaze
And everything of him that touched my flesh.
I rubbed my body from head to toe,
To no avail!
The seed had taken refuge in my entrails.

She returns to the brothel.

I forced the door open and I shoved the brothel owner
I looked for the red room and the red bed
Threw myself into it, and said:
I am pregnant.
She kicked me out of the house, threatened to call the police
And sue me for clandestine prostitution.
I rushed at her, shouting
And you run a brothel without a license!
You recruit minors
Fresh and sealed merchandise
How much for the merchandise, Madam?
We'll keep each other company in the women's prison!

She burst out laughing

BROTHEL OWNER
No way, you're too cute

The brothel of the rich never need a license
You dirty face of misery.

She threw a wad of ten dinar bills in my face telling me

BROTHEL OWNER
Go get an abortion!

I slipped away in silence and never saw her again.

A SHIFT. She is remembering.

For three months
I soaked my feet in a basin filled with hot water and cloves
I drank all kinds of herbs
And with a pestle on my belly morning and night

She hits her belly with the pestle.

Get down!
Get down!
Get down!
Get down!

But it was all in vain.
The seed had blossomed in my womb
And from my entrails
I landed in the bed of a distant clinic
The room was without a door
And the window shattered by the rain and the strong winds.
After nine months less a week
She slipped out from my belly without contractions and without pain.
I warmed her, nursed her, and held her tight.
The silent tears of my life turned into the full-throated cries of a newborn.
That's when the nurse passed by and shouted:

NURSE
Well, there you go!
Go ahead and have your fun
You raise your legs and then you come and whine to me.

Woe to you!
The world swarms with bastards and people sleeping around
And we are surprised that God inflicts a disaster on us every day.
Come on,
Silence your bastard who keeps screaming!

Yakouta
Her name is Yakouta.

I wrapped her in a rag and walked out in silence
The sky was a downpour
I was wading through the mud
She was still crying
The wind abused my body and the movie was scrolling before my eyes—
The red room
The woman
The man I saw for the first and last time—
The diaper got soaked in the driving rain.
Yakouta had turned pale from the cold and from crying
I staggered as I walked out of town
I leaned against a tree.
I put her on the ground without looking at her.
I tore off some leaves
I covered her
And I left without looking back.

A BABY *crying.*

Be quiet…
Be quiet…
Be quiet…
Be quiet…
Be quiet…

I step back

Shhhh

I have a very cute daughter

The Kahia asked for her hand
But it won't be for tomorrow
Even for all of Tunisia, I won't give her away.

She calms down
The wind and the storm cease and the rain stops falling.
She closes her little hand over a lock of my wet hair
And we fall asleep at the foot of the tree
On which a silent bird lands and stays
Until the first light of day.

A SHIFT. This memory recedes. She returns to her HUSBAND.

My husband, I swear, what a fool
He doesn't know how children are made.
He's hitting me and yelling

HUSBAND
How did you get it?!
WHO IS HE?!

He doesn't know how children are made.

Aren't you ashamed to ask me that question?
I am not special.

I had it like all the women who lay children
All the people teeming on earth who were born exactly the same—
From the same concept—
An unexpected encounter with a sperm.
Hence, everyone has in their genes a ferocious animal
And an egg.
A random encounter in time
Between a sperm and an egg.

Scientists and specialists have two versions.
In the first version, it is the spermatozoa that solicits the egg.
The spermatozoa makes himself desired by the egg

By setting his conditions.
In the second version the sperm are fleeing,
And it's every man for himself!
Egg catches a single sperm among thousands,
Opens up,
She cuts his tail and quickly closes in on him.

Spermatozoa all look the same

They're about the same size and composition.
The head is the nucleus, which contains the DNA and the tail.
Although it is true that they all look alike, they are not all the same.

Take Daechian[3] sperm for example.
The egg has barely descended as they start to scream

DAECHIAN SPERM
Allah is the greatest!
Here's the whore!
Fuck her in peace!

And they start cutting off each other's heads with their sabers
As they flee from one another to save their own skin

DAECHIAN SPERM
My brothers why are you killing us like this?
We are Muslims like you!

And one of them,
Ugly as a louse and straight from the Middle Ages, declares

THE DAECHIAN SPERM FROM THE MIDDLE AGES
Nope!
Your Islam is too tender and brotherly
We need a strain of angry Islam
That can slaughter, murder and cut off heads

Like a stick of dynamite that burns in the name of Almighty God

3 Daesh and Daechian refer to the Islamic State, often called ISIS or ISIL in English.

A small number of sperm bathing in all the blood
Eventually reach the egg
And they rape her
And then stone her.

Yet, here's another example
Of how you cannot compare these crazy Daechian Sperm
To Japanese Sperm
Polite, organized, their lines are straight while they wait their turn
The egg
Also waiting
Hand on cheek.
The sperm keeps moving down and up, back and forth.
That's when the egg decides to act before it's too late
Choosing the last in line and flirting with him

JAPANESE EGG
Come on, sneak in
But god, hurry up
Isn't there an Arab among you who can teach you
How to walk out of line??

Thousands of sperm waiting their turn for years
Until the egg reaches menopause.

French sperm:

FRENCH SPERM
Charge!
In times of war we have to make do!
'Arise, children of the Fatherland'[4]

One of the French Sperm is very refined
He delicately swims and hums from the bottom of his heart

REFINED FRENCH SPERM
My egg you're mine, tonight you will be mine

4 Title of the French National Anthem.

He swims
Looks right and left
He's surprised to see all the spermatozoa running to conquer the egg

REFINED FRENCH SPERM
Where on earth am I?
How come there are only Black and Arab Sperm!

A voice answers him:

VOICE
Say what?
Are you talking to me, boy?
We did our part
Our ancestors carried stones with their hands
To build France for you.

(Well, enough with this story now, Manu[5] asked for forgiveness.)

The French Sperm keeps on swimming among the Chinese,
The Romanians
And the thousands of undocumented
It gives him an indescribable rage

FRENCH SPERM
Run François, run Charles!
Is there a George among us?
Oh no, the Yellow Vests[6]
Not tonight, at least let them go through!
We need a purebred Frenchman for this fertilization
Otherwise, we're screwed!

He doesn't even know he's already screwed
American sperm are still in the eternal struggle between White and Black
As soon as the egg descends, it screams

5 Emmanuel Macron
6 French protestors

AMERICAN SPERM
I have a Dream
I Dream of the day when the black egg
Will have the same rights as the white egg
I have a Dream today!

And of course it turns into demonstrations with tear gas
Live ammunition and mass arrests
On the other side a black sperm was passing by quietly
When a white policeman grabbed him and threw him on the ground
Pressing with all his might with his knee on his neck

BLACK AMERICAN SPERM
I can't breathe

For nine full minutes, the white policeman sperm
Continued to press on his neck

BLACK AMERICAN SPERM
I can't breathe

The Black American Sperm died before reaching the egg.

As for the Italian Sperm, they are gentlemen
They deeply care about their wives
They practice hand-kissing and pay close attention to her
And if one of them plays rough, the Italian Egg yells at him

ITALIAN EGG
Ma che fa! Spetta spetta

They like to have fun
And they never stop feasting before they get to the egg

ITALIAN SPERM
Una mattina mi sono alzato
O Bella, ciao! Bella, ciao!
Bella, ciao, ciao, ciao—

Well let's get down to what concerns us

Our blood and our flesh

SPERM OF OUR BLOOD AND FLESH
Who stole the hair gel?
Do you really want the hunk to get there with frizzy hair?
Why are you in a hurry? The egg will think we are chasing it.

Let him hang out, it will do him good
And if he's not happy then screw him.
First let's say a prayer, let's have a little drink
And then we'll attack
Go ahead, pass me a cigarette, I'm dry
Hey, why are you jostling, the egg will not fly away
There is an incredible guy among us
He is a prospector for salt and petroleum
Who managed to bring us the vaccine in a vial of Tiger balm.

A bastard of an egg will not cause him to backtrack
And brother, double check! He must be from a good family!

We want it sealed and with an extra blue cord.
But truth be told, there are exceptional Tunisian sperm!
They swim while whispering

TUNISIAN SPERM
Of all the women in the world,
The Tunisian remain the most beautiful...
Come over here, let me have a little preview

In short, when a woman and a man meet,
They become a threesome with the devil
Nothing happens if the devil is not in the game
The meeting is crowned by the release of an army of spermatozoa,
At attention
And as soon as they hear the shrill whistle
They rush between the surf and the backwash
Cavorting on a water slide
Only having 24 hours to live

They attack
Swimming directly
They go through a canal then through the vestibule
To finally arrive at the patio
This is when they come together around the egg
A single egg besieged by thousands of sperm
Hence the expression "A woman is worth a thousand men"

The egg in its castle has kept its calendar meticulously
Since the first day of menstruation
May God preserve this feminine custom in the name of our holy Saint Manoubia

On the 12th day the ovum dresses up, puts on makeup
And descends into the uterus—
A true night club—
She lights up a cigarette
Crosses her legs and gets comfortable
But that's normal since she has only 36 hours to live
And she has to fight the great army that intends to conquer her.

She pretends to fight
But truth be told, the little cheeky egg takes all her time
To choose someone from a good family
Who makes gifts and spoils women.
While she's making her choice, a sperm tries to impose himself
And the egg turns blue with rage

EGG
Get out of here, you boor!
I saw you with other sperm who sold me out and became traitors
You've teamed up for a (political) Troika
A coalition of destruction

I accuse you!
You are the new monsters
You are Omi Sissi[7] from 2021

7 Popular Tunisian children's character.

Who cut off the tail of my beloved sperm
Omi Sissi, you coward, the egg will never be humiliated!

The sperm got angry

SPERM
SHHHH
Shut up or I'll kick your ass
You are just a woman
And if I didn't exist, there would never be children
Nor a population or filiation
And the human race would have disappeared before the dinosaurs

The egg musters up its courage and exclaims

EGG
I am the egg and you are only a sperm

He grabs the egg by the hair
Drags it all the way through the bowels and smacks it right in the face
This is the decisive moment
The violent moment
When the first embryo is created.
A cocktail of beatings
Hair pulling and spitting
Insults are the extras offered by the house
And you still wonder how we make children!

Since the creation of the universe
We all arrived the same way.
Well—
Not all, there are some exceptions.
Jesus, the son of the Virgin Mary
How was he conceived? Who is his father?
I don't care, it's none of my business
(May the peace of Allah be upon the son of Mary)
How about our father Adam?
He came into the world alone

He was supposed to stay alone in the heavens
But Eve, mother of humanity, crashed in
She was born from Adam's twisted rib and she was only half-human
But by her own will, she made the other half of herself.
May God forgive her foolishness with the apple
What a catastrophe she put upon us
If not for her, we would all be in the Garden of Eden,
Watered, fed and satisfied
Slumped on benches, happy and carefree
It was her fault that God cursed us
Not only did He scatter us across the earth
As enemies against each other,
In addition, he created us unequal in everything
(May God forgive me)
But he gave everything to the disbelievers
The women who are disbelievers?
You would think he created them one by one
With the top of a mermaid and the bottom of a virgin
And the men, oh the men
The size, the elegance
Finesse and silky hair
If only we could have a quarter or a dozen of them,
For a change of taste ...
As for the rest us
When we were created
You'd think he picked us up wholesale
Then tumbled us from the sky
To become the best nation among humans.
Let's recap for those who haven't understood yet.
How do we make children?
On the 12th day the egg descends into the uterus
The sperm swim
Learn to swim
Learn to run
Learn to dress
The egg opens a slit

Cuts off the tail
And it's a disaster

A SHIFT. She speaks to her HUSBAND.

Do you finally understand how I got Yakouta?
Or are you going to keep beating me up to make me confess?
Try to lay another finger on me
And I will file a complaint. Do you hear me?

I said this a thousand times and I forgave you each time
You fool me with a couple of words
Or you make up for it with two very spicy fricassee sandwiches
I forgive you and I shut up.

Do you remember the twenty stitches in my head?
—Not that one, the beating before
You took me to the emergency room telling the doctor

HUSBAND
Doctor, you know the failings of women.
She was mopping the floor in the middle of the night
She slipped on the Clorox
And her head hit the corner of the table

After that you invited me for a bowl of lablabi[8] to reconcile us...

But this time
Even if you were to invite me to that restaurant again
And even if you turned into Antar the invincible[9]
I will refuse to call myself a woman
And I will not run my fingers through my hair
Until
This time I take action
To forgive you.

Come on,

---

8 Chickpea soup
9 Mythological hero

Open the door.
Don't you want to hear the end of the story?

A SHIFT. She is remembering.

We slept another night at the foot of the tree.
The next day
Before the dawn prayer
I dropped her on the steps of a mosque.
I pricked my finger and I pinned a paper on the diaper
On which I wrote with my blood

Yakouta, her name is Yakouta

In disguise, I spent days following her
From one place to another
I felt revived and relieved only when I saw
That she was adopted by a family
With a real mother, not like me
And a father who gave her the most important thing
His name.
I bought her a little plush rabbit
And every day I hid behind an electric utility pole
In front of the house where she lived.
To see her, even from afar, to wave goodbye with the soft toy,
Sending her kisses and telling her ...

I love you Yakouta, I love you

One day I was sheltering behind the pole
The rain poured down and I was electrocuted by 3288 volts!
Since our wires are not well connected, it nearly spelled my demise.
Several days after I came out of the coma
I returned to see her but I did not find her
I was bruised
Sad to death
I looked everywhere, asking people
I learned they left the country

Taking my daughter with them.

Yakouta!

Only after 24 years did we finally find each other
And today we are supposed to meet again

A SHIFT. She speaks to her HUSBAND.

Give me my phone
Give me my phone
Give me my phone
Give me my phone
Give me my phone

At the very least
To warn my daughter that I will be late . . .

What am I going to tell her?
I will tell her I am stuck in traffic.
A visiting VIP blocked the country.
Or that I'm at the hairdresser's
That water and electricity are cut off and my hair is full of dye—
The other day I ran into my neighbor

A SHIFT. She is her NEIGHBOR.

It's been a while since you've come to the beauty salon!
What's wrong?
You're all pale and your eyes have dark circles
Did he beat you up again?!
You're lucky it's only beatings
My husband turned out to be a narcissistic pervert
He poisons my life
Harasses me from morning to night, a real cheese grater

NEIGHBOR'S HUSBAND
Where are you going?
Take off that lipstick, you look like you're coming out of a brothel
I called you a hundred times, your phone is always busy,

Who were you talking to?
You were supposed to be here fifteen minutes ago, where were you?
Who was that guy at the opposite table smiling at you?
It can only be your Facebook lover
Who clicks "like" on each of your posts
The animated GIF that sends red hearts and kisses

The day of the feminist demonstration
He snatched the sign and the flag from my hands, telling me:

NEIGHBOR'S HUSBAND
Liberty!
Equality!
Why're these bitches fighting for this claim?
Did you say queer?!
When the demonstration is attacked by the radicals
You will come to your senses

But the height of humiliation
Is when he publishes a story of the demonstration
Carrying my sign and posing with my comrades
But every time I wear a new garment
Or if I change my hairstyle or put on a little makeup
He will tell me

NEIGHBOR'S HUSBAND
You have become so ugly, following these cheap influencers
Isn't it time to turn to your Lord
Wear the hijab and pray with a rosary?

Have I reached an age for a rosary?
When he has an urge, he becomes cuddly
He doesn't stop kissing me and hugging me
After that, he jumps out of bed like a madman
And bombards me

NEIGHBOR'S HUSBAND
You are disgusting,

You make me vomit,
Everything about you horrifies and sickens me.
You cow, you suck, you're stupid, you're ugly.
Shame on you if you think you're a woman.

They say it's a variant of love
But me, here I am swallowing all the antidepressants.
Sometimes I want to jump from the roof
And smash myself into pieces,
Or open my veins in the bathtub—
The water would take on the color of my blood.
I bought candles and petals
And a white nightgown that I hung up
At least I would have a beautiful suicide, just like in the movies.
But I am cowardly and resigned,
I silently swallow both sweet and bitter
I cannot do otherwise.
I am submissive, it is my destiny. I'm a woman.

A SHIFT. She is an INFLUENCER.

You are a woman
You have to be perfect
Like the "influencers"
The ones at the heart of every topic, for TV ratings and creating buzz
You must be like them
Dress up, stretch your eyes, put on false eyelashes
And lenses to give your dull eyes color
Inflate your lips so you never run out of kisses
Add a hair extension for long locks
Or treat it with keratin to have hair smooth as silk.
You have to nourish your face with all the masks
To hide the wrinkles of shame
And dye your roots every fifteen days
So you're not humiliated by your grey hair.
You don't have to be too thin or too fat
You have to be thin and-slash-or fat

Slender but plump
A flesh that melts in the mouth and in the hands.
And if you're too poor for plastic surgery
To remove belly fat and bounce your butt
You just have to wear a girdle that takes your breath away
To hide the folds and pleats of your belly.
You'll slip your feet into high heels
You can't walk with
On your arm a fake designer bag
Dark glasses on your sore eyes
And you are no longer you.
But this is beautiful.
You will look at yourself in a mirror
You won't recognize the woman you see.
You will smile and shut up.

A SHIFT. She is a traditional, working-class COUNTRY WOMAN.

You are a woman.
You have to get up in the morning to bake the bread
Then climb into the back of the truck
To earn your day and feed your husband who sleeps at home
And your flock of kids.
You scratch the ground, your back is bent, your face scorched by the sun,
Your hands are scratched.

A woman arrives in a big black car.
She offers you a box full of food
A bottle of frying oil, a bag of flour and a pack of pasta
She speaks to you with the intonations of "your dialect"
While toasting a cup of red tea
To the health of elections and to your poverty.

At sunset, you go back to the back of the truck
After paying the broker and the driver.
You start counting the few pennies you have left
When the truck skids off with the twenty workers.

The only thing left of you is your scarf fluttering in the wind.
And that scarf will become fashionable
And it will be sold for ten times more
Than your daily wage, for which you died.

Your husband is going around in circles not knowing what to sell
To feed the kids you left him

A SHIFT. She is an 8-year-old DAUGHTER.

He sold his 8-year-old daughter to a broker of a maid service
Where she became a sleep-in maid in a huge villa
And did everything with her little hands.
When she would find herself alone,
She would run to her little mistress's room filled with toys
Her eyes falling on the blonde doll in the pink dress
That smiles at her
Without even knowing that her name is Barbie.

When her day is over she goes to bed
In the maid's room at the end of the garden
She embraces the cold and lets herself be lulled by her silent tears.

The wife of the villa owner is in a depression
So, every other night, the owner goes to see the little one.
He offers her a piece of chocolate with hazelnuts
He takes the little girl in his arms
And talks to her about his misfortunes, his concerns,
His business, his lover
And about his wife who he hates and who he can no longer stand.
She listens to his stories
The barking of the dog in the garden,
The cries of her mistress who is having a fit
And she keeps silent.

The first day of each month
Her father shows up to collect her salary
She meets him at the gate

Gives him a bag full of hazelnut chocolates
That she collects for her siblings
And asks about her twin sister Hsaina.
While crumbling the bag in his fists her father responds

FATHER
When we got up this morning we discovered your sister's body
Hanging from the tree in the courtyard.

She tries to speak, but he grabs her by the neck—

FATHER
What's next, the hanged eating chocolate?
Did your master give you anything else?

She suffocates between his hands
She keeps silent.

A SHIFT. She is a SECRETARY.

You are a woman
You've been working for the same administration for years
In the same office and with the same salary.
You bring a file to your new boss
His hand accidentally touches yours.
With honeyed eyes, he asks you to close the door

POLITICIAN
What is this perfume?

It's called enticing the other, sir.

POLITICIAN
I swear on my girls' heads, I got goosebumps
How long has it been since you got a promotion?

Your former boss recommended you and the promotion is approaching

POLITICIAN
Come massage my neck

I have a stiff neck from bending over the interests of citizens
Yes ... Go down a bit more, press again.

You massage his neck
And under his neck
In silence.
You leave and collapse at your desk and you concentrate on your work.
In comes the handyman of your boss,
He throws your pantyhose at your face

HANDYMAN
You forgot your "file" at my boss' office
Your boss ... He puts his hand to your hair,
So I too have the right.

You pick up your things and leave in silence.

You take the subway home
A boor rubs himself against you from behind
The subway rolls through one of the working-class neighborhoods
Where you live
A bedroom, a living room, a tiny kitchen,
The toilet is integrated in the shower, and the hot water is cut off.
Your husband has dinner and sits in front of the TV
Waiting for you to finish the housework, the laundry and the dishes.
You lie on the bed and fall asleep from exhaustion.
You feel something sticking to your body ...
Is it your old boss or your new boss
Your boss's handyman
The subway passenger
Or your husband that you left in front of the TV
Surfing for porn ...
Against your will, he forces you to satisfy him

HUSBAND
Marital rape is not called rape
It's a matrimonial right.

He'll take it when he wants, as much as he wants
And you keep silent.

A SHIFT. The same SECRETARY *is now at home.*

You are a woman
Yes he beat you up, big deal.
You think you're better than Refka and Chahinaze?
Both murdered by their husbands like thousands of other women?
Be thankful that you are still alive.
You know he's short-tempered, why do you get on his nerves?
When you see that he is not well and in a bad mood,
Especially when his favorite team has just lost a game,
Swallow your emotions and stay away from him.
Don't show him the electricity bill.
Don't tell him the toilet is broken
Or else you'll be drowning in shit up to your neck.
Don't show him your daughter's report card
If you don't want him to knead you both like pancakes.
And why do you let your hair grow?
So that he can grab it and drag you from the living room to the tiny kitchen
And to the toilet integrated into the shower where the hot water is cut off?
It's because he only calms down when he pulls a tuft of your hair.
Get a boy haircut then, it's fashionable
And you will also save money on hair products
A doctor's note?! Are you going to file a complaint?
You idiot!
You fool
Go ahead, do it, who will hear you?
They will take turns ridiculing and humiliating you.
Your husband disfigures you, makes you bleed, bruises you
Draws a rainbow around your eyes
And you have open stitches everywhere.
And even if you became Frankenstein's monster,
You have to forgive him
Even if he doesn't apologize
In fact—

You should be asking for his forgiveness
For the beating you deserve for your rotten life.
You have found a husband and you are being difficult!
Dirty whore
Take good care of him
He is a man that many other women envy you for.
Look at the pious sisters
Who demonstrate
Demanding the return of polygamy
So that their husband spreads his sperm fairly
On his four legitimate wives
Sharia law gave him this right

A SHIFT. She is a PIOUS WOMAN.

And why would you deprive him of his right?
My sisters, how can you accept that you are becoming an old maid?
Share your spouses and may Allah bless you.
This will be counted as alms for good health
And a good deed saves you from the tortures of the grave.
When the two friends (angels of death)
Come to knock you out with a blow to the skull, the blow will be light.

A SHIFT. She is yet ANOTHER WOMAN.

My sister, to find serenity
You have to get up six, seven, ten times a night
To tuck in your husband who is sleeping
With his legs apart and his arms open
Leaving you a tiny space to sleep.
You have to lift his head and ensure he has a quiet snore
Just so you can take a nap between two of his snores.
Of course, while he's wrapped in the duvet like a sausage
Make sure he's well covered
In order to avoid harmful gases to his heart.
And if he has a nightmare and starts screaming

HUSBAND

Farhouda, don't leave me alone, I love you my Farhouda, I love you!

Give him light massages while reading from the Quran,
The chapter called Yassine
Don't even ask yourself who this Farhouda is
He may love her or he may die of his love for her,
His nightmare is none of your business.
After this sweet night of happiness, you will get up at dawn
You will wash your face, brush your teeth, and especially comb your hair
So as not to frighten him and make him think you're a witch.
You will prepare him a good breakfast
With boiled eggs, sorghum, various nuts and sesame paste
To strengthen his knees and his punches.
Tiptoeing, you will wake him up with a whispering kiss
Sweetheart.
Just once.
You know what awaits you if you dare wake him up a second time.

Your master and lord wakes up with a crooked head,
Shuffling and scratching.
You really understand everything about him,
Except the fact that all men scratch themselves when they wake up!
He sits down to eat even before freshening up and washing.
Heavy drooling, eyes swollen and half-open,
Hair disheveled like a hill borrowed from *Hourya Sunday*[10]
His whole head is like two parallel lines that never cross
Who don't cross paths for real
Unlike those "two old guys"[11]
He starts eating while you shine his shoes
And after ironing his shirt.
You walk him to the door, your head bowed, you throw tender words.

---

10 Creation Resist'Art 2017—Musical-theatrical show written and performed by Leila Toubel with the Franco-Tunisian artist-composer Mehdi Trabelsi.

11 Referring to late former President Beji Caid Essebsi, who joined forces with Rached Ghannouchi, leader of the Islamist Ennahda party, against the will of the people who voted for him.

He ignores you, doesn't answer you.
No "thank you" nor "goodbye."

What? A kiss?!
What's wrong with you? Have you lost your mind?
Your role is to be the slave of your husband
So that he leaves home serene and ready for the vexations of his boss
The boss who stole your husband's mistress.
And to take revenge on his boss, he builds a case from scratch
With embezzlement and conflicts of interest.
Through all of this, you have only one role:
To assume your marital duties
And you keep silent

A SHIFT. She is yet ANOTHER WOMAN.

Do you think you're a woman?
Your husband comes home after a hell of a bad day
God alone is his witness.
He finds you with a witch's head
Smelling of Vicks and throwing up, having a migraine attack
What did this husband do wrong
To have to face such disaster when he comes home?
Then you complain that he abandons you
To spend the night with his mistress.
But of course he will go to his mistress!
At least at her place he finds laughter, appetizers, tapas and crazy dances
When she gets drunk, she messes around, daring to be vulgar
He will be laughing hysterically

HUSBAND
Stop it my slut, my beloved whore
You are too funny
May God protect you, my one and only Farhouda

How long has it been since your husband laughed with you?
You should tell him a joke
Tickle him, dance for him, clown around, do the monkey

Impersonate a deputy with a motorcycle helmet and a loudspeaker[12]
Take a walk and come back to him the next day
After he rejoices with Farhouda.

And not just that!
Go around and come back to him at the end of the month
To give him your full salary in cash
Doesn't he deserve it?
Isn't it better that he gets drunk with it
So when he comes back he won't beat you up?
You're not thinking of spending your salary on feminine futilities, right?
Clothes from thrift shops, perfume, lipstick, hair salon,
And going out with your girlfriends?
You give your salary to him
You give your salary to him
You give your salary to him
And you keep silent.

A SHIFT. She is an ELEGANT ACTRESS.

She is a beautiful girl of eighteen
Her body is completely fulfilled
Proud of her youth and her beauty
She dreams of becoming a big star.
She spends hours in front of a broken mirror
Practicing walking the red carpet
Waddling in her mermaid dress,
A necklace of rhinestones around her neck.
Striking a pose in front of cameras
And photographers screaming her name
Eyes dazzled by the brilliance of flashes and lights
And a fake smile glued to her lips

DIRECTOR
What a beauty!
Your lips are made for the role

12 Refers to a female Tunisian MP.

And the main sequence will be filmed in the dark
Turn off the light and dance
Again and again
Not bad, that's good.
What a beauty!
Keep going
Wonderful!

She dances for him.

And now you're going to show me how you run away from the dark
Throwing yourself into my arms hiding your fear
This role, miss, will take you to the top
Go up a little more,
Throw your crazy locks at my face
So I can make sure that you are well suited for this role.

She didn't get this role, nor the one after, nor the next.
She did all of her casting between one bed and another,
For both women and men.
Here she is again
In a mental asylum.

A SHIFT. The ELEGANT ACTRESS *is now an* ASYLUM PATIENT.

When they take her out into the flowerless garden,
She looks for the face of the sky
And poses in front of the crazy people around her
One of them is playing photographer ... *Click click!*
"One more, not bad, this is good"
No, let me dance, the role will be played in the dark
Don't chain me to bed
Don't make me swallow pills
I want to dance.
Don't ask me to shut up
Don't ask me to shut up
Don't ask me to shut up

Don't ask me to shut up
Don't ask me to shut up
Don't ask me to shut up

A SHIFT. She is yet ANOTHER WOMAN.

A little girl who came into the world
When they were expecting a boy.
They gave her a name
And called on a pious man to pray in her ear.
They wiped her navel and swaddled her feet
To protect her honor.

When she turned five
At nightfall,
They invited Omi Halima, a pious woman.
She confiscated her doll.
With a razor blade, she made seven cuts on her thigh
Soaked seven raisins in her blood and made her swallow them
Asking her to repeat

OMI HALIMA
I am a wall and their son is a wire[13]
I am a wall and their son is a wire

Seven times
Omi Halima tied the secret word in her scarf
And reassured the girl's father and mother

OMI HALIMA
Your good reputation and honor are preserved
Her virginity is guaranteed and assured
Even a battalion will not be able to deflower her
Until I utter the secret word over her.

Since girls are seeds of the devil
She grew up fast and a man asked for her hand.

---

13 To be a "wire" is to be rendered impotent.

After two years of being deprived of the sun,
The week of the wedding arrived,
And for seven days and seven nights
The Hanana[14] fattened her up while asking her to repeat after her

HANANA
Oh my luck, my lucky star
Give colors to my cheeks and swell my forearms
Oh my luck, oh my lucky star

Seven times

A SHIFT. She is a BRIDE.

On her wedding day, the mother went to Omi Halima's
To invite her back and say the secret word over her daughter, the bride.
The neighbors told her:

NEIGHBOR
Don't you know?
Omi Halima has Alzheimer's
It's been seven days since she left and she still hasn't come back.

The mother came home upset, with a dry mouth
She whispered in her daughter's ear
Leaving her in her nightgown in her bedroom

MOTHER
Oh, what misfortune and what bad luck!
I can no longer joyfully ululate!

The GROOM *enters. The* BRIDE *addresses him.*

Hello—
Wait, slowly!
No foreplay? No kisses?
Don't push me, be patient—
Wait, let us chat!

---

14 Beautician

Omi Halima,
Who built a wall so no one can deflower me,
The poor woman has Alzheimer's and forgot the secret word.
So you will remain as the wall and I, the wire
No, you're the wire and normally I'm the wall.
Oh, the walls of our house are so pretty!

The groom's gaze hardens

GROOM
What are you doing to me here?
My father, my mother, the sheikh, my brothers,
My cousins, the neighbors, the relatives
And all the others are waiting for the proof of your purity!

Only them?
Try and remember, isn't there anyone else?

Just kidding!

I should have kept my mouth shut...
This moment does not lend itself to laughter—

Wait, let me explain.
You are indeed a man, so you must be the thread
But now let's try again.
You say seven times I am the wall and you are the wire

But why are we doing all this?
Check your sex organ with your own eyes.
If you determine that you are not the wall and you are not the wire
Do with me what you want.

I am indeed your sister—
I mean your wife.

Look how beautiful I am. Let me seduce you.
My cheeks are walls
And my arms are red over indigo blue

Remind me, who said "don't call my party indigo blue"?[15]
God bless my indigo darling.

Honor ... I am ... Me ... Omi Halima ...
Hold on ...

She has a realization.

I am a woman
Okay
I'll keep silent
I'll keep silent.

The groom smashed her head against the wall,
Leaving her like a thread on the floor.
He walked out with her bloodied shirt
And was convicted of honor killing.

Honor killings number in the thousands.
Blood that washes off dishonor is not a crime,
The law condemns it only a little, if at all.
How many women are killed each year,
By their husbands, lovers or partners?
How many cases of rape and attempted rape?
How many Yazidi women were sold by Daesh for 10 dollars?
A woman trades for between $10 and a pack of cigarettes,
So that the terrorist commissioned to cut the throat of an innocent
Or blow himself up killing dozens of people around him,
Is sated
And is not distracted by the excess of his own sperm.
How many girls between eight and nine years old are sold as slaves
And become the property of their masters who rape them?
And once they've had their fill, they pass them to the sons
Then to the driver
The gardener
And even to the guests of his house.
How many girls are forced into marriage before the age of twelve?

15 Refers to the color of the Islamist party in Tunisia.

To this day, little girls continue to be circumcised.
We butcher the labia minora and the labia majora
Or the entire reproductive system
In order to abolish all of her desires, her pleasures and her enjoyments.
A rotten instinct in order to avoid any chances of scandal.
How many women are trapped between dark walls?
Their silent tears scratching the soul and the cheeks
How many?
How many?
How many?
How many?
How many?
Because you are a woman.

A SHIFT. She is a WOMAN IN A DRESS.

Tell them the story Omi Tfila ...
When at night, your brother slips over your body
You keep silent

When at night, your father deflowers your body
You keep silent

And when your cousin, back from your brother's wedding,
Desecrates your body
You keep silent

When your uncle abuses you while you sleep at his vacation home
You keep silent

And when it's your stepfather and his son,
Your grandfather and the owner of the villa
You keep silent

When your son damages your 90-year-old body
You keep silent

When you get harassed by your new boss and your old boss
By your boss's handyman and the guy in the metro

By your teacher and the religious man
Who teaches you the Chapter of Women in the Quran
By the cop and your coach
And the comrade who invites you to have a drink to teach you activism
You keep silent

When you're raped in the red rooms
In slums or castles
In a deserted place or in the marital bed
You keep silent

And when your husband burns you alive
And you watch him with your eyes open
You keep silent

And for any act of a male possessed by the sperm in his head
You keep silent

And in his knees
You keep silent

And in his spinal cord
You keep silent

And in his thoughts, his words, his saliva,
His fist, his honor and his manhood
You keep silent
You keep silent
You keep silent
You keep silent
You keep silent
You keep silent because you're a woman.
You keep silent because you're a woman.
You keep silent because you're a woman.
You keep silent because you're a woman.
You keep silent because you're a woman.

A SHIFT. She is yet ANOTHER WOMAN.

How long will we light candles
Shall we lay roses
Will we change our profile pictures
And maintain our social media accounts?
Each new victim added to the long list
Is an opportunity to gargle with numbers.
Statistics are good
We write press releases
We protest, take selfies
And we go home happy and satisfied.
To prepare dinner for the Mister,
We wear a sexy nightgown
Hoping for a little tenderness from him.
Thousands of girls and women arrive
With a face, a body, dreams and a story
And they end up in oblivion, without a future.
They become statistics and silent graves.
According to the farthest corner of men's brains
A woman's honor always lodges between her legs.
A body created to be consumed.
A craving like a bite of stuffed pepper
A fillet of veal
A chakchouka with dried meat
A cutlet, a sausage, stuffed tripes
A cold slice of watermelon that cools his ardor in the afternoon heat.
She remains the major reason for temptation
She ignites man's instincts
And he has every right to empty his bag of sperm.
Do you want him to explode?
It's up to you to cover yourself up to avoid being raped.

Cover yourself.
Because look at how beautiful you are like that.
A well-covered, well-dressed, desirable black shade.
Well, not exactly…
This way, you won't be desirable anymore.

Cover your body, don't dress in a miniskirt
Don't go out at night, don't stay late
Don't drink, don't smoke, don't flirt
Don't dance, laugh, or talk out loud
Look down, don't claim your right
Don't think, don't dream
You must be a straight-forward fool
Who follows the path that has been traced for you.

A SHIFT. She is yet ANOTHER WOMAN.

You spend your life in silence, fearing people
You are afraid of making a mistake
Afraid of yourself
Of your body, your feelings and your desires.
You're so scared that you miss the first train
Then the second, then the tenth, until the arrival of the last train.
Death descends from the last car
She smiles at you and says

DEATH
Finally, girlfriend! It's time to leave,
The whistle of the last train has sounded.

DEATH *says something to the* WOMAN *that we cannot hear.*

What do you mean? Why did you change your mind?

DEATH *says something to the* WOMAN *that we cannot hear.*

No, it's just that your sister Life is a liar
For all my life, she danced, winking at me and telling me

LIFE
Enjoy! Life is beautiful, look how beautiful I am
Enjoy me to the fullest

And then she knocks me out with a fatal blow.

I get up and she does it again, even harder.

Why did you, Death, become as big a liar as her?
We had an agreement on everything.
And you promised me in *Solwen*[16] to kill me with a patriotic heart attack.
You changed your mind, didn't you?
Because I'm a worthless woman.
I let myself be beaten without reacting
And now you are depriving me of the death I choose.

An enormous SHIFT. She is addressing DEATH,
but she is also addressing us.

You have no right.
I claim the right for myself to die, to be shot and to be flayed
It's because of this damned country,
Abused in broad daylight by politicians
Who violate the slightest grain of sand
And every part of her body.
For ten years they killed all the beautiful things in the lives of the people
They slammed the doors in the face of spring.
They slaughtered all hope,
Smashed boxes of love, trampled bags of dreams
Uprooted cyclamen and burned flowerpots.
And what nerve
They insist on appearing, threatening, discoursing
When they are the cause of all misfortunes, ruin and disaster.
We are citizens who share garbage food with cats,
Hospitals without beds and without doctors,
Without scanners or medicines,
The elevator floating between heaven and earth.
Children washed away on their way to school
And money stolen by rampant corruption.
And sleeper cells and terrorists, disguised in a suit and tie
They will explode when there is a crisis.
Roads are rutted and valves of wealth closed.

16 Creation Resist'Art 2015—Monodrama written and performed by Leila Toubel.

Open sewers that engulf Farah depriving her of life.
Youth holding a menu, hesitating on the choice of their death
A rope, an immolation or in a cell,
Jump into a boat and drown offshore
Or a beautiful sexy death, as it has been called.
We've been through it all
And there's only one small step left till starvation
With the helicopter circling above our heads
Throwing us sacks of rice.
But it turns out the merchandise is Turkish
And since we are very proud and we care a lot about our dignity,
We'd rather die than eat this rice!
We hate you so much and we hate your words and speeches and—
Who is the YOU?

The cunning of wolves behind your smiles.
Your bulging belly, fattened on the backs of the starving.
Your faces with a thousand masks.
We hate your bickering and your vulgarity
Your insults, your lies and your turpitudes.
Your junk coalitions, your tricks and your haggling. Your tangled belts.
What else are you hoping for?
You sold the country and brought it to its knees.
Because of you, it's desert and ruins.
And you still have your mouth wide open?
Hm ...Hm ...
Choke on it.

May God deprive you of your sperm, all of you, without exception.
I hope the next time you wake up,
Your channels will be as dry as a desert.
You will never be able to defeat us.
Women will get on your nerves, grill you and brown you in an oven pot
We will confront you and make your life a rollercoaster.
In March and in the four seasons
We will stay here in spite of you.
And we will hold with all our strength

This country that you have torn down
And I who am nobody, who am in front of you
I am ready to become a pimp.
I will sacrifice myself for my country by playing the matchmaker
I will coordinate the meetings between sperm and eggs
By ensuring a romantic atmosphere
A candlelit dinner
And a sauce of languorous kisses served in music.
I will create harmony between their hearts
So that from the first embryo to the fetus
Which, remember,
Is created from punches and hair-pulling
And is the source of our misfortune
So that it becomes a cocktail of love, humanity and patriotism.
And let any gigolo dare to silence me.

A SHIFT. She speaks to her HUSBAND.

You see saw what happens when you lock me up?
I have a fit of claustrophobia
I become delirious and I unpack everything in bulk.
From Yakouta, I digress completely.

May you be cursed on earth and in the hereafter!
Come on, open the door
Otherwise I'll throw myself out the window
And even if I'm broken to pieces, I'll go out to see my daughter—

She escapes the locked room.

Ever since we found each other
I've counted the days and I've dreamt of this reunion ...
Come hug me like that night we ran away from the clinic
And we slept under a tree.

Yakouta, you are the worst and best thing that happened to my life
I am sorry for not having lived with you
For not having been present at the push of your first tooth

And to not have celebrated the event with sugared almonds and sweets
I didn't change your diapers and smell your big poo
I didn't celebrate your first birthday
I didn't dress you in a princess dress, my princess
Nor a cake with one candle, singing to you alone
Happy birthday, my Yakouta
Alone, and then
As if I were ten, twenty, one thousand people!
For your fifth spring, I would have bought you raisins
From the market souk El Fekkah
I would have called on Omi Halima
To prevent a battalion from deflowering you—
But I'm not crazy!
I would have demanded the secret word before she left.

Yakouta, I didn't teach you the lessons of life
Nor how to protect yourself and preserve your honor
I didn't forbid you to put on the perfume
That awakens their uncontrollable desire.
Luckily, you're not married yet
I'll give you a big wedding with the right songs—
But what a fool!
I forgot that I don't know how to ululate.
When they play my favorite music
I'll start waving and dancing barefoot
And the mother of the groom will be mad with rage
Her only son turning away girls from good families
To fall in love with a bastard
God alone knows what Yakouta made him eat.
The groom's father will join me in the dance
He will hold me by the shoulders with lust in his eyes
The mother of the groom will have a fainting spell
And the evening will end in drama.
Then you'll go home to a working-class neighborhood
A bedroom, a living room and a tiny kitchenette.
Before the end of the year you will get pregnant

You'll come to me, blood sticking to your hair from the beating you took.
I'll send you away telling you
He's your husband despite everything
Shut up and swallow your tears
Choke on it and preserve your household.

She begins to SHIFT.

My darling, my heart
What if we went on a reality show like *Only Truth Matters*
They would put a bucket of foundation on us
Soak our eyes with a product to make us shed fake tears
Mascara will run down and we'll tell our story

She is YAKOUTA'S MOTHER ON A REALITY TALK SHOW.

I'd like to thank you
And thank your show
The owner of the TV channel
The initiator of this program as well as the whole team.
To be honest, we were very well received by you.
I want to thank the fashion designer who dressed us
And who put a hashtag #dressed_by
On Facebook, Twitter, Instagram, Google, Yahoo...
I also want to thank the make-up artist for the make-up and disguise
So that no one would recognize me
Even if I called half of Tunisia
To let them know I'll be on TV.
I thank our live audience and those who are watching us at home
After bombarding them dozens of times with teasers
Between the ad "Our strength is in our spicy harissa"
And "A cow for everyone who no longer laughs"
I am very happy to be followed by thousands of viewers
Thanks to my mother who tangled her hair and prayed
So I can spend my life putting on this show.
Those who watch us will have a great evening
And will love our sad story

Women will be outraged
"May God preserve us from scandal and gossip!"
And men will present their gratitude to God
Because their mothers, sisters, wives, daughters
Neighbors, cousins, mistresses and Farhouda
Are all the fruit of Halal sperm.
The show host will ask me my name
I will proudly answer
Woman
My name is Woman
And today I'm going to tell you my story . . .
A mother who found her daughter Yakouta after 24 years

And I will add that I have cancer
And that it is fun. I swear it's going to be hot!
And 12 million Tunisians will cry their heart and soul out.
He will ask me

HOST
Who is the father?

The father is a sperm, a single spermatozoa

HOST
Madam, look at the camera
And tell us
What message do you want to send
To the millions of viewers who follow us?

What camera? This one?
Oh, that one
I want to tell the viewers ... I want to tell them ...
Emotions suffocate me
So give me a glass of water

The show host screams

HOST
STOP!

The HOST *calls cut and stops rolling.*

I am the one who must ask for a glass of water

The HOST *resumes the show.*

That's not crying
Where are the tears?
You are not crying for real, Madam
Do you want the thousands of people watching us
To realize that this is only a masquerade?
Let's start all over again!

Start over what? I started over ten times already
You've exhausted me.
Do you think I have a button to press when I need to cry
You're the one with buttons!
When you take orders from your bosses, you do it.

They squeezed more product in our eyes to get tears.
Everything becomes blurry.
He turns to you

HOST
Yakouta
This woman who is your mother
Dared to abandon you in front of a mosque
When you were only three days old
What do you want to tell her
In front of the millions of viewers watching us?

YAKOUTA
The first thing I would like to say to my mother...

A SHIFT. Everything recedes as she returns to being herself, a WOMAN.

What?
Your name is no longer Yakouta?
But I pinned the paper on your diaper with your name

Written with my tears and my blood
Who changed your name?
Who took your name away?
They have no right to erase your name
You will remain Yakouta despite them
Bastard, damn them all!

But you are Yakouta
Your mother is a whore
Your father is an X...or Y or Z
But the origin of all the letters are sperm
Vomited by a man into the bowels of a woman

You are Yakouta
Whether they drag you through the mud, get you dirty on the ground
They can rape you or enjoy seeing your blood between your legs

You will remain Yakouta!
Don't hide your tears
Don't be ashamed of your laugh
Don't cover your body, don't stifle your desire
Love yourself! Love every part of you!
And don't let any man ruin your life
Don't be perfect or imperfect
Be you. Get off the rails, get out of control, mess around.
Make mistakes, be crazy, have fun
Cross their red lines
Rebel against their traditions
Rise up against their laws
Denounce their hatred and their contempt
Face all those who want to say
SHHHH
To you
And speak up, even if the whole world comes together to silence you.

Live, Yakouta!
As if you were the joy and the colors
Live like a butterfly that doesn't burn in the fire

Like a flower garden
A sturdy palm tree that a tsunami could not move
Like a bird that dreams at night and leaves the nest at dawn
Yakouta, you are the roots of this land
Under which the martyrs sleep
And above, you are the motherland.
Don't be afraid of the sound of silence, of the color of darkness
You are the candle for dark rooms
And the sob of silent tears
Because you are a woman
La Donna
The Lady
The Woman
La Mujer
And all the women in the world are rubies.

Shhhh
Be silent…
Yakouta is talking!

Uprooting

or,

The Dog and Cat Pizza Chapters

By Sami Nasr

Translated by Jonas Elbousty

ON *UPROOTING*

Sami Nasr's situation-horror-romance-comedy *Uprooting; or, The Dog and Cat Pizza Chapters* is a heretical mystery in the shape of funhouse. The plot moves like a document of uprising, laden with jaded jihadists, nihilistic entrepreneurs, and low-level rulers of limited power. The landscape is ripe with beguilingly discordant imagery. Right and wrong function as shadow nodes from another time—which may itself be a false memory. Consider the opening of Chapter Three:

> *The morning is a broken piece of meat. Time is a rusty plaque. There is love, and ten frail chickens scratching desperately in the dirt. There are some desperate trees where a few blind birds are hopping back and forth, and in the distance, a river leans on its nesting banks. There is fear that has grown wings, claws, and canines. A faint sobbing can be heard in nearby neighborhoods.* FAIQA *and* NAHAR *are talking, indifferent to everything else.*

A sense of egalitarian romance is blossoming in the ruins. Faiqa and Nahar are political twins, navigating a rotten state that has nearly snuffed out any possibility of love. They might seem to offer the possibility of a boy-meets-girl (or girl-meets-boy) narrative under precarious conditions, but Sami is too sober, curious, and incensed a writer to believe romance can fix all. These are sharpened humans—Nahar and his eventual accomplice Faiqa are (spoiler) cat killers, after all—and they live in an atmosphere of chronic corruption, even if the oft-invoked nation goes unnamed. As the lovers plot their next moves for survival, poetry and violence disorientingly mingle in the space between them and their ravaged land. The combination seems destined to explode at any moment. For me, an ethical question emerges: am I at home in this body of language or have I traveled far away? Can I call it a home? Or do I, with my learned western liberal impulse to find the universal in all things, do it a disservice to see my own life in the work?

One resonant collision: Gender is a cage and a joke between these primary navigators, Faiqa and Nahar. At a certain point in *Uprooting*, the lovers discuss the possibility that they might become one in their love, only for the fantasy to arrive quickly at a dreaded masculinist conclusion: "Mercy! God forbid. Become a hermaphrodite? Good God! God forbid."

Everything in this play seems to sour as a brutal mirror of life lived under authoritarianism. What hurts most is the way that "the authority" gets inside us, curdling the spirit and making police of each of us. The play's final image wonders if there is not something ecstatic in self-destruction. It forces me to fathom that disillusionment possesses the force to extinguish life. Every death, even in ubiquity, changes the world.

— Jess Barbagallo

CHAPTER ONE

—Uproot it. Just uproot it. Why do you care about that shit? Tear it out by the veins. Throw it on the ground. You'll feel much better once you uproot it.

—What should I be uprooting?

—The sky. Uproot it. You'll feel better the second you get rid of it.

—Better about what?

—The dirt, the smell, the rusty nails. You'll notice her legs, those shapely thighs, white, like diamonds. You'll see her like a maker, not a buyer. You'll see her navel, round like a pomegranate flower. Pour in some wine and drink. Take it easy. Drink the wine that mingles with her sweat. See her stomach rubbed with frankincense, sprinkled with crushed mint; her dewy back dusted with flour and scrubbed with cloves. So what if they're poison? Burrow into the irises that grow between her thighs, and gaze from there towards the horizon—the ancient, shaggy cypresses that lie in her shadows.

—All that, and I missed it? I didn't see any of that! What I saw was ugly. Ashes. I'm frightened by ashes. The veins of the sky are dry, black, etched in the air. I could never rip them out by the root. The ones before me tried and got exhausted. They failed miserably. The sky is a black tree—bloody, foul, festering. A corpse. Who cares about corpses? Who cares?

—Just uproot it and be at peace. It won't take more than an hour of your time. It's in bad shape. Don't be fooled by her blue color and the few stars scattered across her back; the sky's an old ruin, rotten from the inside. As old as the earth. Leprous. An aging woman whose body is marred by scabies. Destroy her—she's cursed. And be at peace. How long will you leave her as she is? How long will you keep looking at her and muttering prayers to the prophet? Uproot her. The sky's the oldest building on the face of the earth. Once she's gone, you'll finally and truly see the world!

—What will I see?

—Close your eyes and touch her. Touch her. Her flesh is fresh and alive: a neck like an ivory tower, eyes like pillows that cradle her nose at sunset, and breasts… what can I tell you about them?

—Tell me, for God's sake, tell me!

—Breasts like ivory.

—Keep going…

—Twins, like sleeping partridges.

—Yes.

—Breasts like the teats of twin does.

—Yes!

—Breasts like two blossoms, heavy with clusters of fruit.

—And I didn't see anything! All I saw was darkness.

—I told you to uproot it. Then you'll see everything. You want me to tell you how?

—Please.

—Start with the roots that have already decayed. Uprooting those is easy. The roots planted in mosques, political parties, and the media. The worm-eaten roots, the dry-rotted roots. When you uproot those, you'll feel relieved.

—You'll help me?

—I'm too old! I spent my life shaking the ivory tower of her neck, shaking the unshakeable. Milad, son of Monji al-Sawaf, he filled the pools of her eyes with tar. He doused the light that used to blaze day-in and day-out. Sliman al-Jilali, son of Bornia, owner of the Turkish bath, he sliced off both her breasts and threw the nipples in the fire. Fadel, son of Jamia, the weaver, spun a bed across her belly-button like a spider and from underneath he dug out the flesh. But now she's a crumbling building—only real men can handle her.

—So where are those friends of yours?

—Milad was poisoned. Sliman was found chopped to pieces in his own house. Fadel is still alive. But they skinned him and shattered his bones. I'm the only one left.

—Her nose still points toward the homeland.

Who's speaking?

A nose smeared with blood.

Who's saying that?

Sword blades are her hair. Blades dipped in blood. An endless night are her locks, dripping with poison.

No one and everyone!

The dock-workers, their noses severed, sing to her: How beautiful you are! How sweet, beloved! And when she turns away they mutter: You whore! You're lodged in our ribs like rods of iron, and what's left of your breasts oozes pus and infection. O eternal prostitute, there are no clusters of fruit left in you. O consort of evil, O you who change truth for falsehood.

—Don't be fooled by her violence. Believe me, she's all aches. Yesterday, I saw Nouri, his wife Fadda, Miloud Elhajjam's wife Yasmine, and his aunt Fattoum all sneaking into the space inside her ribs. There are no solid ribs left inside that snake. They're all turned to birds, sheep, and horses. I left her for good. There's no bed inside that woman, no birds, no fish. She's empty, I'm telling you! Don't you believe me?

—And where are they now, the ones you just mentioned?

—She crushed them, just like that. She let them creep in, and then she crushed them between her rocky hands. The river's pebbles heard their screams. She was more than happy to pour their blood into her temples. As for their flesh ... well, she still has tigers in the old temples, too.

—So you want to see me dead.

—I want you to start with her veins. They're her weak spot now. Her breasts have veins, her grapevines have veins, her clusters of fruit have veins. Her wine—wine of the finest quality—which courses secretly through her veins—pour it out. Don't fight her in the cities. Fight her in the wide wilderness. Track her through the villages, watch her among the trees, in the falling rain, in the lightning storms. Step back from her and you'll see she's smaller than she seems, and meaner. Her lips are scorched clay, and her fangs dipped in black poison. She may smell like apples or pears, but it's the smell of corpses. What you want, sir, is in the veins. All her evil is in the veins. All her poison.

CHAPTER TWO

The sky is a skullcap. People are dogs. The desert is poison, mounded into sand. A YOUNG MAN *appears. He holds a living cat and presses it to the wall with one hand. With the other he grabs a hammer. He holds a thick nail against the cat's stomach and starts hammering. When the nail is midway in, he stops. Coldly, he holds another nail against the cat's neck. He hammers, slowly but determinedly. The* OLD MAN *enters. He sees, but is unfazed. The* YOUNG MAN *approaches him. The cat is crucified against the wall, its blood dripping to the ground. The two busy themselves chatting.*

—I hate cats.

—I do too.

—They want me to be white. I hate myself when I write about whiteness. That's why I use my hammer and nails. I feel better when I pound them into the flesh and the blood starts dripping. If I can't drive nails into coffins, I drive them anywhere else. Yesterday, I drove nails into a rat, and before that a rabbit. You can see—here. I've got plenty of nails and a hammer, but their heads are still elsewhere!

—Idiot. It's not their heads that need hammering, it's their veins. Where there are veins, there should be hammering.

—I'm training my hammer and nails. Each dawn I wet their points with blood.

—You say their heads are elsewhere. But they're becoming rulers now. They have everything. In the mosque they told us that there were so many of them they were going to start collaborating with our former rulers. And we're getting cut out of the deal.

FAIQA *enters. She sees the cat, takes it down from the wall, tosses into the corner, and wipes the wall. She sits close by.*

FAIQA
A fat cat. Goddamn cats!

OLD MAN
With each cat, one of them is killed. If only killing them were as simple as killing cats.

YOUNG MAN
My hammer has a soul now, and my nails are becoming conscious. Yesterday I tramped through their blood. I'm neither the rose of Sharon nor the lily of the valley. They filled the valley of my childhood with disgust. It's still filled with disgust. My soul is riddled with thorns, Faiqa, and I have no beloved among the girls.

FAIQA
We need to *dig*. We don't need hammers, we need shovels.

OLD MAN
I lost all my apples—what will I do with my life? They stole my children. They said they had no trouble with us, just with our children. You're right. We need shovels, not hammers.

YOUNG MAN
I'll be done with the cats soon.

FAIQA
There's no end of cats.

OLD MAN
They prepare a place for me in the shade of the fig trees, with my children. They tell me there's sweet fruit here, and they tempt me with rivers of wine. They say, You gain nothing, antagonizing us. They promise me white garments and raisins, and they prepare virginal maidens for me. They swap my old apples for the fresh apples of their tender breasts.

FAIQA

And what do they prepare for people like me?

YOUNG MAN

My cousin Moncif, the son of my aunt Monjia—they chopped him up under the olive tree. They promised him the same thing as they promised the old man, then snatched his soul from his body. They killed Sulaiman Talil and crushed al-Eid, Youssef's son, the owner of the mill, to dust. For those like you, Faiqa, they're preparing an eternal darkness, obscurity without end.

FAIQA

There's no solution but to uproot them. The hand placed beneath my head is severed, and the hand draped across my body is smashed. I don't want anyone to embrace me. I don't want anyone to warn me. I don't want anyone to compare me to the moon, the doe, or the gazelle. And I don't want anyone to think of me as soil for planting children or stars. There will be no owls shrieking and no crows nesting in my mountains. I don't want to be protected by a man or a text or a contract or anything. My mother bore me free.

OLD MAN

They took our texts, daughter. They took our country, and everything became theirs.

YOUNG MAN

I still have my hammer in my hand. I don't need their flowers, their branches, their doves, their curves, their vines, or their figs. What do I need with what they have? One day they'll fall under my hammer and my nails will pierce them.

FAIQA

Isn't there another solution?

OLD MAN

No. None.

YOUNG MAN

The solution is hammer and nails.

FAIQA
The solution is shovels.

OLD MAN
As night falls we need to dig deeper. There's poison planted everywhere. There's darkness, there's bottomless fear, and there are corpses. The sky becomes a broken skull, discarded under the feet of people who have become vermin. Yesterday, I heard about humans who had turned into fleas. Others turned into worms, others into maggots. With my own eyes I saw people who had turned into lizards and chameleons. But most of them had become fat cats and dogs.

The OLD MAN *goes, leaving the* YOUNG MAN *and* FAIQA.

FAIQA
They brought him back in a coffin. I woke to find him dead. They killed him like a dog. Nothing left but the faint echo of his voice. We hear him all the time, in the flap of every wing. We see him leaping in the mountains and jumping in the hills. Sometimes we see a small deer struck by a hunter's arrow, or a gazelle caught in an abandoned trap. Other times we see him in the house's front window, standing, peering through the glass, calling to me.

YOUNG MAN
Help me!

FAIQA
Who, me?

YOUNG MAN
Who else? They killed Milad. I saw his abandoned corpse. He spent twenty days baking in the sun. What am I supposed to say? How would I even say it?

FAIQA
No one can uproot it. Generations have tried. But there she was, spreading her arms, extending her wings, her fangs sharp and filled with poison.

YOUNG MAN

I spoke to her a few days ago. I told her: I don't have anyone but you. In you are all my seasons, your rain never ends, your warmth gives and gives. You hang on my back as wings and cling to my chest as flowers. You grow on my mind like basil, like climbing flowers, like grapevines. In the land of my memory I hear your countless voices. Really. I told her that. I said it all, and my heart was a ripe fig, my heart was heavy with clusters of grapes! But she didn't hear me. The dawn visitors had come before. By the time I arrived, she was trampled, her vineyard spoiled, and her spirit defiled. She was my lily! And I was the guardian of the lilies. Now the days stretch out ahead of me, lined with corpses, under the eye of the sun. My shadows are filled with worms.

FAIQA

They killed her, too?

YOUNG MAN

I don't have anyone but you now.

FAIQA

And I no one but you.

CHAPTER THREE

The morning is a broken piece of meat. Time is a rusty plaque. There is love, and ten frail chickens scratching desperately in the dirt. There are some desperate trees where a few blind birds are hopping back and forth, and in the distance, a river leans on its nesting banks. There is fear that has grown wings, claws, and canines. A faint sobbing can be heard in nearby neighborhoods. FAIQA *and* NAHAR *are talking, indifferent to everything else.*

FAIQA
I never found him. Not during the day, and not at night. I dreamed of him, and I asked for him the way the Sufis ask for their hearts' desire. I spoke to stones, floated through markets and alleys, made deals for apples; I cheapened my body, I undervalued it. I spoke to people, urged them, Tell me! But nobody listened. In the old city the watchmen found me, near the gold market, among the potters, on the Qarous hill—they found me lying on the ground. They offered me water and fed me. They told me, Listen, daughter, you mustn't do this to yourself. They don't know that I hate it. It happened anyway. I asked them, Have you seen Ritocho, the one I love? But they didn't answer. They didn't know. They abandoned me on the road. They left me alone.

NAHAR
Were you crazy?

FAIQA
I'm crazy now. I was sane before. I found him crucified. I went to him, hanging there, and I grabbed his legs. I told him, I love you. They heard me and said, Wake up, fool. And I woke up. I started seeing shadows, flying overhead with black wings, and when the big shadow got close, it became human. I saw him crucified. It was as if I was holding his legs, telling him I loved him. He wouldn't reply. But

listen—sometimes I think he's still alive. I feel that he's descending, lowering himself to earth, and embracing me. I'd hold him hard, climb all over him, bring him to my room and my mother's room.

NAHAR
You slept with him?

FAIQA
Of course I did. You don't believe me?

NAHAR
Your fantasies are real, and your reality is fantastical. I don't understand you.

FAIQA
(*Laughing*) You're jealous. You want me only for yourself. Do you like my body?

NAHAR
(*Surprised*) You're crazy. I swear to God you're crazy. What are you saying?

FAIQA
(*Stunned*) All you do is break up with me and leave. Cats are your life's obsession. But the fat cats—are you sparing them your hammer and nails?

NAHAR
You're right. I never found anyone my soul loved. But that's not so strange. What did I ever find? Voices scream inside my head, along with texts, gazelles, deer, and hyenas. In my skull, an unfeeling world boils, and columns of smoke rise—often they turn into people—scented with frankincense and bitterness. Each of the ones I don't love—underneath stand sixty tyrants, an imam, a reciter of scripture, and some new ruler with his divine mandate. Under their robes, I catch glimpses of sword blades. I see blood, crushed bones, and burnt intestines. Out of nowhere, a monster appears among them. Its head is not a head, its body not a body, its eyes not eyes, and its feet are not feet. The world around it changes suddenly. Then the monster speaks:

O people, I will rule you. I am the shadow of the Lord, obey me. And you see them bow down in submission.

FAIQA
Our imaginations are similar. Do you think we'll ever succeed in anything?

NAHAR
I want you to give me a son. Maybe our child will manage to change something. But us ...

FAIQA
I'm pregnant! Pregnant, Nahar. Will you raise him as your own?

NAHAR
Raise a bastard? God forbid.

FAIQA
There's a cat inside you, Nahar. That's the cat you need to impale on one of your nails. I'll raise my own child. His father was hanged days before we could sign the marriage contract.

NAHAR
You don't look pregnant! Damn you. Your reality is fantasy, and your fantasy reality. Damn you!

FAIQA
The monster is making a kingdom for himself, and you and I are just strays among the ruling felines. Do you see the silver pillars he's made for himself, now that he's demolished the copper market? Do you see the golden roofs he's built, where the shantytowns used to stand for the homeless? The throne draped in purple. The streets paved in gems and rubies. The palaces filled with Faiqa lookalikes. In every house now I hear your hammers and your nails—being driven into all the wrong places. They need to land in the monster's head. Strike the head. The roots are in the head. As for my body and the rest of me—they're yours. I'm not pregnant, no. Not at all, you fool. My lover wouldn't do it. When you become my wife, he said, I'll make you pregnant. I never managed to become his wife.

NAHAR
Forgive me. I don't have anyone but you.

FAIQA
I forgive you. I don't have anyone but you.

CHAPTER FOUR

A working-class coffee shop. Three men are gathered. An OLD WAITER. *Horses in the back. Bare trees and a harsh wind. We hear a soft and monotonous moan.*

QUADER

Why remember? It's better to forget! If they let us go, we should thank God we survived.

TALIL

You think they let us go? You're out of your mind. Their eyes bore into us always. Our families are hacked and so are our phones. I feel them sleeping in my bed. He says forget! Impossible.

RABEH

I returned to an empty home. It was while I was in their prisons that they buried my mother. Same with my father. I lost my job and my wife. If you want to forget, I don't blame you. But you can't forget forever. For a while we forget them—and pray to God they'll forget us too. But alas!

The OLD WAITER *brings the tea to the table. He glares at their faces with his usual stare, then drags his feet down the long corridor.* FAIQA *enters. She throws her bag on a chair near where the men are sitting, orders tea, and starts twisting her hair into a bun on top of her head.*

QUADER

I think she's one of them.

TALIL

They always pick the pretty ones. Look at her. Her eyes are like two startled doves.

RABEH

You say her eyes. You're talking about her chest.

TALIL

Look at her hair! It's like a herd of goats in yesterday's pastures. Her teeth are frozen clusters of hail, and her lips are crimson ropes. Her mouth is sweet, her cheeks are pomegranate halves, and her neck is a tower. Such beauty—and you say she's theirs?

RABEH

They'll leave her neck and crucify yours with ropes and guns. You'll end up hanged or shot. Their dogs will take turns tearing into that flesh you love so much. Look at her breasts. She's not breastfeeding, she's too young to be a mother. But still—she looks used-up. This Sawsan has had her whole chest consumed. The spirit of the gazelle has been snatched from within her. The light in her eyes has been snuffed out.

TALIL

In her eyes you can see a slaughtered day, defeated shadows, and mountains of frankincense and bitterness—charred and scentless.

QUADER

But she's beautiful. She's flawless.

RABEH

Give me one night with her. Then they can kill me. My death would be my life. If I could have her, I could even manage prison.

TALIL

You're right, Rabeh. You're right. She looks like our country—without sin. Still—doesn't she look exhausted from all these curs, strays, rejects? She looks like a bride, but trashy, too. Do you think she'd come with us?

QUADER

All three of us?

RABEH
All three of us! Unless you, sir, aren't interested?

TALIL
A smile from her would be enough for me. If I could just make her smile. But she's sad. If sadness were a man, I'd murder him!

QUADER
Kill your own sadness first.

RABEH
Someone should talk to her. I forgot how.

QUADER
And I don't feel great.

TALIL
And I...

The café remains a hollowed-out skull full of stray mutts—with their lingering eyes and their bared teeth and claws. The OLD WAITER *is a creep, a well-known snitch, who serves with nothing but scorn and disdain. The chairs are tired and worn.* FAIQA *finishes her coffee and glances at her watch. Eyes follow as she stands and heads toward the door.*

QUADER
She's abducted my mind.

TALIL
And I'm enlightened!

RABEH
She seems ordinary. Maybe we read her wrong?

QADER
(*After she's gone*) Now we're just three bags of shit! How disgusting! A bunch of geezers. Ugh.

MASKED MEN *enter, armed, and open fire. The three bags of shit erupt, spilling out across the floor, a mix of entrails, shredded flesh, excrement, and blood. The* MASKED MEN *slip out silently, quick as they came, monsters in their eyes. They barely register their victims.*

MASKED MEN
God is great!

ECHO
God is great!

QADER
(*Dying*) I wanted to tell her, You're sweet. I wanted to forget my sins with her and then repent them all over again. I wanted to bring her to the country and take her to see my grandmother. (*He groans deeply, in pain.*) I wanted to tell her: With you, I could be the way I used to be. With you, my heart could become a heart again—caught the way hearts get caught. I could see the world through my heart's eyes, and be happy. I wanted to tell her, I want to die with you.

He breathes his last.

TALIL
(*In the clutches of death*) No one ever knew me. I lived deprived, and I died deprived. My love is sweeter than wine, but who has tasted it? My scent is honeyed, but who has breathed it? I passed through life unnoticed—unnoticed by people, unnoticed by God! I was forgotten. No one knew the honeycomb of my mouth, the milk and honey under my tongue, or the smell that wafted from my chest—the smell of my homeland, carried off by the wind. (*He groans as the three bullets pin him to the ground.*) I die, a locked paradise, a sealed spring, a closed uterus, a blocked fountain. My seedlings, my eden of pomegranates, my fragrant fruits, my spikenard, my jasmine, my maple, my almond, my plum, my reed, my cinnamon, and all my blossoms—they have withered on their branches!

He tries to speak, bleeding profusely. He works through the thought, as his spirit slips from his body like a flayed snake—resisting a little, then plunging into pools of blood.

RABEH

(*A bullet in his chest*) Now I can rest. The wind of my breath has stopped completely. But the breath of God—tossed into the hands of the mad—now *it* must stop. No one heard me. I came in silence—and here I am, leaving in silence. (*He remembers lines he memorized and believed in once, reciting them in pain, his voice rising with strange laughter.*) *Awake, O north wind!* Ha ha ha! *And come, O south wind!* Ha ha ha! *Blow upon my garden...* Ha ha ha! *...that its fragrances may pour forth!* Ha ha ha! *Let my beloved come to her garden*! Ha ha ha! *And eat its precious fruit!* Ha ha ha!

No one hears him as he slowly dies.

CHAPTER FIVE

The hammer is on the table and there are nails everywhere. NAHAR *is standing behind the window, gazing at the horizon.* FAIQA *has been daydreaming. Nailed to the wall are fat cats from the city and lean ones from the countryside. Some are still dripping blood.*

FAIQA
With a verse they kill them, and with the same verse they bury them: Glory be to God!

NAHAR *doesn't say anything.*

The one who killed them yelled: God is great! And the one who'll bury them will yell four times at top of his lungs: God is great! Truly truly, O Nahar, we're a blind nation. We can't see reality anymore.

NAHAR
Enough of blindness. I've got an idea—a great one. I'll tell you on one condition.

FAIQA
What's your condition?

NAHAR
The condition is that we become one person.

FAIQA
Become one person! You mean we get together?

NAHAR
No, no, I mean we become one body—you and I. We'll have two eyes and one mouth—who needs two? Two legs, one belly, two ass-cheeks, one neck.

FAIQA
And one head?

NAHAR

One head and one mind. You and I will become one. Why would we need multiples? If they killed you today, we'd die together. Wounded, our blood would flow from two ancient banks. Two histories, two sorrows. If you leave, I'll go with you—that's what will become of our differences ...

FAIQA

(*She smiles, then laughs flirtatiously*) You mean that you love me! I know that. I already know you love me. Why talk about it this way?

NAHAR

That's my condition, if you want to hear my idea. Let me in, or I'll let you in. Dissolve into me or I'll dissolve into you. I won't say anything else unless the condition is fulfilled.

FAIQA

(*She calms down. The condition seems strange to her.*) If we become one person, should we be female or male? Honestly, I don't want to abandon my femininity.

NAHAR

I don't want to abandon my masculinity either.

FAIQA

What kind of freak would we be if I stayed a woman and you stayed a man?

NAHAR

Mercy! God forbid. Become a hermaphrodite? Good God! God forbid.

FAIQA

So why do you want to become one person? I thought that was your condition. This is your battle, Nahar—not against them, but against yourself. I'm starting to think you're actually just like them. Hermaphrodites—you think people like that aren't human beings? Or maybe you think they're unwell? It's not the street cats that should be killed; it's the cats roaming your own mind.

NAHAR

You want to be a male hermaphrodite? You think that's normal? What kind of miserable life is that?

FAIQA

I didn't create them. And I have no right to say a word against them. If you really want me to dissolve myself in you, you'll have to let my femininity into you—not erase it. My light, dear one, is ancient, and there's a hidden world inside my body that no other body knows. Become a part of me, and I'll have you dwell in spirit, where there is no gender. Your body will be a shell, no more. You'd refuse that?

NAHAR

Refuse what?

FAIQA

To dissolve yourself in me and I in you! Become a third sex!

NAHAR

Mercy! God forbid. Isn't there another way? Some alternative?

FAIQA

So drop the condition, and let's hear your idea.

A MAN *enters, wearing butcher's clothes. His features are severe. He's livid.*

MAN

Why would you make me wait all this time? The sun's been eating my head. May God's curse be upon these damned times we live in!

NAHAR

What do you want?

MAN

When are you going to bring them out?

NAHAR

What do you mean, "them"?

MAN

The longer you take to get rid of them, the longer it takes for us to butcher them. And if we're late to butcher them, the whole operation gets delayed! It's a shame and a waste. Why would you change the schedule? May God's curse be upon these times!

NAHAR

I didn't understand a thing you've said.

MAN

The cats! Weren't you the one bringing them out every morning? What's taking so long today?

NAHAR

My cats? What's wrong with them?

MAN

Allow me to introduce myself. I'm Dali, meat collector at Dog and Cat Pizza, out in the suburbs. There are twenty of us, and we come around every day, collecting any dead and discarded cats, any chickens left in dumpsters, any carcasses tossed out on the road, any stray rats. You don't recognize me?

NAHAR

(*Perplexed, dumbfounded*) Dog and Cat Pizza is feeding us dead dogs, cats, and chickens? Who the hell do they think they are?

DALI

You were expecting beef? It's called Dog and Cat Pizza. Why are you surprised? You're the one murdering the nation's cats. It's reckless and deranged. And you're mad at me for feeding you a little wild rat meat? You're supposed to be as wild as they are. Curse you and curse your parents. When are you going to toss out your trash?

NAHAR

My trash?

DALI

I don't have time for this. Is there anyone sane I can speak to?

FAIQA

Give ten minutes. I'll collect them for you. I'm sorry for the trouble. Ten minutes!

FAIQA *collects the cats, as she does every morning. She piles them in a cardboard box and brings them to* DALI. *He peers inside and looks pleased with today's catch. He loads the box in the backseat of his car and drives off.*

DALI

Bring them out early tomorrow. I don't want this to happen again. Damn these sinners—the country is full of you!

FAIQA *reenters, wipes the hammer, and stows it in another thick box. She collects the scattered nails, closes the box, and hides it deep in the closet. She approaches* NAHAR. *As usual he's at the window, staring off into the distance.* FAIQA *looks dazed. She watches the souls of hundreds of cats fill the room. She watches their blood drip from their spectral ribs.*

FAIQA

We've done something shameful.

NAHAR

We didn't kill the cats. It wasn't the cats I was killing. Can't they understand the metaphor in what I say and do?

FAIQA

We're all to blame. They're the ones who should die. Not their shadows, and not their cats. If we tear out their veins, their metaphors will die. Otherwise we'll end up in a mental hospital. Dali's right.

NAHAR

You trust the guy who collects dead rat meat—and you don't trust me? You don't trust yourself? Damn the time we live in. I almost want to drive the last nail into my own skull. But no, not now. I need this head. For now at least I need it. And it needs you, too. Without you, Faiqa, I'm nothing.

FAIQA
And I'm nothing without you.

NAHAR
Whoever abandons his metaphor dies. Without a metaphor, we die like stray dogs. We end up eaten by the customers at Dog and Cat Pizza.

FAIQA
But we're alive, dear Nahar! Who needs metaphors?

NAHAR
Let the cats live, then! Sure! Why not? So all this time, we were wrong. Dali was right. Nahar and Faiqa were mistaken. Damn life and damn its victories!

A TV screen in a back room drips blood. The announcer bloviates, but no one understands the news. No one elected the ones taking power, but still—this is democracy! One monster has become Speaker of the House, a second was voted President, and a third has been appointed Prime Minister. Countless monstrosities, their fangs shining in the shadows, are sharpening their swords.

NAHAR
If the condition isn't met, the idea won't be spoken.

FAIQA
Understood. No condition, no idea!

NAHAR
Have you memorized any poetry?

FAIQA
What, now?

NAHAR

Now's the best time for poetry. I'm afraid I'm losing my mind. How awful today is! Recite some poetry? Maybe a little poetry will change things.

FAIQA *recalls an old poem she used to know by heart. It's something her lover used to read to her. She speaks it slowly, imbuing it with an ageless sorrow, her eyes worn out, as around her blood continues to trickle from the spectral ribs, and the room fills with the smell of monstrosities.*

FAIQA

You are my dear one, my beating heart, the blood in my blood.
You are my love, the fragrance of my country, a question in my mouth.
Sweet, he is my secret and my madness. He is my very self and being!
If only your stars could grow, my evil would be wiped away!

You are my dear one. Near or far, it doesn't matter.
Absence cannot remove you, nor can estrangement pull you away.
You are in my thoughts. My age, my voice, my life.
You live in my pulse. Under my skin. Inside my bones.

It's not love, all this love, it's not love at all!
It's not adoration, this adoration, no—it's no great passion!
It is a bottomless gift. It is endless songs.
O how I love you in my now—in the folds of my dream.

You are my dear one, my end-time, my last chance to live free.
You are mine. We are wings—yes, wings—and I was once a mare.
Bring me to the light—fly with me—and I will cross universes, O sweet one, soft as a thought.
Take me. Fill my being with hope. Be at ease with me ... Hold me and be at ease.

NAHAR

How sweet these words! I don't know the poem. Who wrote it? Is it what I think it is?

FAIQA
What's your guess?

NAHAR
I'd guess it's his poetry. You lover's. I hear he was a poet.

FAIQA
Poetry couldn't save him. They flayed him alive the way Dali butchered your cats. They crucified him. He died standing.

NAHAR
His words live.

FAIQA
You're right. His words live and move. Have you had enough? Or do you want me to keep going?

NAHAR
Keep going. Keep going...

She summons her man's voice as she recites. She recalls the day he recited it to her in Bar Belkacem Etarifi—she recalls every touch and flirtation.

FAIQA
For whom, this mad and rebellious passion? Answer, O my heart!
For whom this love plunged like a knife into a vein! Is this normal?
This sweet spring...this carelessness...and all my prayers and supplications...
This expanse, which stretches like forgetting across my soul and my flesh ...for whom?

NAHAR
They skinned him alive?

FAIQA
And crucified him.

NAHAR
I'm asleep, but my heart is awake. Let me into you—let me dissolve

into you—or let me bring you into me. Paradise is inside you, my sister, the very tree of paradise. You're the sweetness and the bitterness—you're the honeycomb. I can be your female, you can be my male, one body, no differences. No more differences. Not ever. Open for me. O my sister, O my love, O my dove, O my wholeness, they've filled my head with mud, they've drenched my body with the dew of the night.

FAIQA

This isn't your text, no, these aren't your words. What's happening to you, O dear Nahar? Are you delirious?

NAHAR

You're my robe. I couldn't take you off even if I wanted to! You wear me, O Faiqa. Your leg is my leg, the dirt on yours is the dirt on mine. My hands extend into your hands. Your wounds have become my wounds. Your guts are my guts. We're no longer separate.

FAIQA *is taken by what he's saying. She looks like a bat in a burning nest. She speaks of her husband. Her eyes are squeezed shut. Her mind is a scarecrow.*

FAIQA

I opened my heart to him, and erased all the differences between us. I pressed my soul into his over and over, and the pregnant clouds dripped their perfume and incense all over his fingers. Yet he left me. He walked away. O, Nahar, I've been slaughtered so often. My soul has fled so many times—the light in my heart has dimmed. Standing beneath him, as he hung there, I told him, I love you. But he didn't hear me.

NAHAR

Your past presses on you. It doesn't matter. The dead are fighting me for you. It doesn't matter. No one else will take you from me. You're me now, you've accepted the condition!

FAIQA

You agree, then—we'll become a third sex?

NAHAR

Didn't you say people like that were made by God?

FAIQA

Yes, you think I made them myself?

NAHAR

I agree. God is merciful. For your sake I agree.

FAIQA

If the condition is fulfilled, the idea gets shared. All you have to do now is tell me your idea.

NAHAR

My idea?

FAIQA

Yes, your idea.

NAHAR

I have no idea anymore. Just you. There is nothing in my life but you.

FAIQA

O, my love.

CHAPTER SIX

Thick-bearded men pass in a hurry. Others with lighter, carefully-trimmed beards pass with caution. Still other beards—neglected, trimmed, or thick on the bottom and thinned on the sides—pass quickly. Extinguished eyes. Dangling hands. Blood, clotted into the form of a massive cloud, confronts FAIQA *every morning as she leaves home. Yesterday, two hands, severed at the wrist, fell on her while she was walking. Two days ago, a male organ landed in front of her. Two weeks ago, she watched children playing with a human skull—eyes shut, tongue silenced, and skin intact, like tanned leather. Night is a needle!*

FIRST MAN
We don't know when?

SECOND MAN
Maybe today or tomorrow. Eventually our turn will come.

THIRD MAN
We'll die like dogs in a foreign country, but at least we'll have some fun before we go. They say Syrian women are wonderful—like women in Paradise. We'll get our share of Syrian women.

FOURTH MAN
They sent our wives ahead of us for sex and left us behind. How I wish I could give my soul and body to God, like my wife did. But God wills as He pleases.

FIFTH MAN
I don't have a wife. They trained me to be a wife. They said they could use my ass to store ammunition, or give the fighters some relief. I ache for it. I ache for Paradise.

SECOND MAN
(*In a whisper*) You're not just a cuck, you're a fag too? You send your wife to fuck with those criminals? And you sell your own flesh? Shame on you, shame.

(*Out loud*) They gave me ten million. They said I'd be a leader in the organization. So I paid a year's rent, settled all my debts, and left the rest to my mother.

THIRD MAN
They charged me with enough crimes to keep me in prison twenty years. They said I killed, raped, counterfeited, traded weapons, and stole. There was no felony I didn't commit. They told me Islam would forgive whatever was past. I told them I'd done it all—everything but act a cuck or a fag. They told me it was best if I stayed in prison. So I agreed. But then they all took turns with me. They sent their wives to mine to convince her to leave me. They asked me to divorce her. They swore God would give me a better one. So I did, I divorced her. And they took her and used her to quench the passions of the martyrs.

FOURTH MAN
(*In a whisper*) I'll bring her back. God willing, she'll be alive and ready to forgive me. My flesh stinks. They all accuse me. And what for? Just for a bit of money?

(*Out loud*) *Jihad* is the obligation of every Muslim, man and woman! May God strengthen us and deepen our faith!

(*In a whisper*) Death and punishment to whoever issued that ruling, and to whoever legislated this disgrace. May God blind him, deafen him, and rot his flesh like he rotted mine!

FIRST MAN
They told the butcher boys to finish their training. They said they'd pay them later. The day before they travel—once the Turkish visas are ready—then they'll get their money. To the guys from Sidra, the Western Quarter, and my Uncle—may his soul rest in peace—they said, Memorize the Quran and entrust your bodies to us. Your bodies

belong to God, and we're its guardians. Whoever accepts is welcome. Whoever doesn't either keeps his mouth shut, or we'll shut it for you.

(*In a whisper*) Anyone who speaks out dies. No games. I said yes. I agreed. I sold my soul. I was ripped apart. They did unspeakable things to my flesh. They made me hate my own body. They sucked the life out of my mind. Quran and destruction—all at once. Atrocities are being committed in the name of religion. I asked myself a thousand times why I accepted. Why did I sell my soul? Why did I agree to things even an animal would refuse?

(*Out loud*) Our passports should be ready next week. It won't take any longer than that. I'm looking forward to the virgins. I want to die a martyr.

They look around in fear. The fear never stops. An old rust runs under their bodies. Groups of bearded men hover around them. Veiled spirits. Veiled hearts. Exposed backsides, passed around by the beards. Frightened young boys, accompanied by their families, pass by. Some girls are draped in black, with no sign of eyes, mouths, chest, or the slightest flicker of life. Frightened chickens. Dead cats. Piss fills the air. FAIQA *appears.*

She walks calmly by, and sees the men. She doesn't care. She likes shaved men better.

CHAPTER SEVEN

Men are wearing veils. What's the wonder in that? Horses with only their eyes exposed. Goblins and bulls hide behind dark fabrics. Even the trees have draped themselves in dark garments that obscure everything. Tigers, lizards, and mantises breathe heavily under their veils. The whole world is being tugged towards an inexcusable void. FAIQA *is almost naked. Her chest is two fat doves nesting on a marble rod, and her behind is a balcony that overlooks two vast mountains. The cats that she has started to see recently are only the littlest bit afraid.*

FIRST VOICE
(*Sings—eyes shielded in darkness*)
There is nothing of you left for me to remember,
You and time are both gone.
You were with me when my heart was yellow,
But today my heart has died!

SECOND VOICE
There is nothing of you left for me to remember,
Besides a trace of pain, smothered in blood.
You look like a statue,
Unaware that love is poison!

THIRD VOICE
(*Finding itself, with force*)
There is no joy in you
Only one wound that grows inside another.
What did you imagine? That your clouds
Could drown my dream?

FOURTH VOICE
I refuse history.

I refuse its event and I refuse its torture.
I refuse its beating, its strikes, its violence.
History is indelible,
a tattoo.

FIFTH VOICE
I won once.
Mostly I lose to pain
You are a swarm of crows.
You bear no sorrow.

MASKED MEN *multiply. The market is crowded. There are gasps of admiration and chagrin.*

FIRST WOMAN
Twenty dinars! Even twenty dinars is enough! Hell, I'll do fifteen. I need milk for my babies. God have mercy.

SECOND WOMAN
Take your time. Look, see, check me out. Touch me wherever you want to touch me. Just bring me somewhere clean. Let me sleep in peace tonight!

THIRD WOMAN
Two days for the price of one. Three days for the price of one! That's a steal!

The market is a colony of ants.

FIRST VOICE
Nobody's buying.

SECOND VOICE
The songs are getting old.

THIRD VOICE
And the verses from the Quran?

FOURTH VOICE
Their market is booming. They have a parliament now. A prime

minister and a president. They even have monsters to protect them!

SECOND VOICE

They've drafted a law on zakat for us. And soon they'll draft a law on jizya! Do they think we're dhimmi? They think we're prisoners of war? Slaves? Ha ha ha ha, I heard them talk about canceling the personal freedom laws and reinstating sharia.

FIFTH VOICE

I heard them say, Wherever you find them, kill them.

People are gathering, their faces covered in dirt, with eyes hardened like clay. Tree vines overtake all the squares like a curse.

A GIRL

(*From behind her veil*) Tell me some sweet words! Ugh, I'm tired of your coldness!

A BOY

A few months from now you'll be my wife. What do we need words for?

A GIRL

Say, You are most beautiful among women. My heart needs you. Say, I'll go down to your paradise, O woman. Wherever your fragrance spreads, there I'll live.

A BOY

Shame on you, what kind of talk is this?

A GIRL

(*Thoughtfully*) There are clusters of lilies between my thighs that have never been touched. There are grapes in me, multiplying inside my breasts. My breasts are pomegranates that no one has handled. I'm beautiful as a sunrise that no human has ever seen. (*She removes her veil*) Tell me I'm beautiful, like a balcony suspended over a river! Tell me I'm as monumental as the homeland, as formidable as an army flying its banners! Tell me anything—you're killing me!

A BOY
What are you doing? What kind of foolishness is this?

A GIRL
(*Hopeful still*) Tell me my eyes are two rivers approaching eternity. Reach out your hand and touch me, don't you like my hair? When you look at my body, don't you see stallions sprinting in the desert? Stretch me out here in the market. Lay me down in front of everyone. Look! Don't you see me? My cheek is a slice of pomegranate. All these years I've kept it for you. Use your hands and peel it. Peel me in front of everyone. Suck me, seed by seed.

A BOY
You've lost your mind! Have you no shame?

A GIRL
(*Calmly*) You're not the one I want. You're exhausted, your eyes are drowsy, your nose is stuffed, your hands are leaden, and your soul is a ruin. If you can't see the moon in your lover, it means you're blind. And if you don't feel any desire to enjoy her and make her enjoy you in front of everyone, it only means you've never loved her. I'm going. I'll seduce the first stranger who reaches for me. I'll seduce him and spread my harvest between his hands. I'm awake as the morning itself. There's a vast and boundless universe inside my body. A white sun blazes and blooms in my soul.

A BOY
May God bring me someone better than you!

A GIRL
You have no bounty and no pomegranates. Your seasons never bloom, and your valleys are dead! Maybe now you're gone all my worries will go, too. Goodbye.

She disappears into the crowd, her hijab thrown on the ground, her lips gashed with wound-red lipstick, her eyeliner perfect. Her stockinged legs push her powerfully forward through the mass of people.

The MUSICIAN *tunes his oud. He seems indifferent to the people around him. He waits until his friend sits down beside him. He begins playing after she starts to sing.*

The SINGER*'s eyes linger on the* MUSICIAN. *An ancient longing hangs from her body. Her voice moves deep and soft.*

SINGER
I dream of you becoming rain
And soaking my windows
My sobs are heavier than rain
When I think of you!

The MUSICIAN *repeats her words. His fingers flit across the strings of the oud like blue butterflies.*

SINGER
He folds himself in the hands of others
Forgetting about my hands
I fill the cups of others
But who will fill my cup?

Men, horses, monsters, and bulls. The trees themselves are dressed in deep black, no part of them visible. Tigers, wild beasts, and panthers breathe heavily. The whole world is afflicted with absence. As before, FAIQA *is almost naked—her breasts are two fat doves perched on a marble rod, and her behind is a balcony that overlooks two vast mountains.*

NAHAR
I'm scared!

FAIQA

Fear is normal. I'm even more scared. But there's no other solution.

NAHAR

The trouble is up there in the sky! Not here on earth. The earth is fine. Our trouble isn't with God, it's with the ones who rule with God. I've got no issue with the sky.

FAIQA

The solution is to uproot it. Uproot them.

NAHAR

I've uprooted it from my mind—but them ... How can I uproot them? Uprooting the sky is easy. They're the problem. Uprooting them is hard.

FAIQA

Just tell me one thing.

NAHAR

What?

FAIQA

Tell me you'll uproot them. Don't tell me how or when. That's all I want.

NAHAR

I'll uproot them. I have to. There is no solution but to root them out.

CHAPTER EIGHT

NAHAR
Your breast, I want to suck on your breast.

FAIQA *exposes her chest, and hands him her right breast.*

FAIQA
Tell me it's bad. Tell me it's no good. No, no, don't bite. No biting. It hurts.

NAHAR
When do we get married?

FAIQA
I'm already your wife. The rest doesn't matter, the rest is just stupid details, I don't care about that.

NAHAR
Good. So slow down and talk me through it: when do we finish the details?

FAIQA
Reach your left arm under my head and hold me with your right. My breast isn't going anywhere. Hold me between each suck. There's no God but God! What witchcraft is this?

NAHAR
The witchcraft of wine, mingled with pomegranate juice.

FAIQA
Where do you come up with these things?

NAHAR
You made me a poet.

FAIQA
And your nails? And your hammer? I worry you'll forget.

She tucks her breast back inside her wool shirt and buttons it. She looks into his eyes.

Do you love me?

NAHAR
No other man could love you the way I do!

FAIQA
The others, the others, the others—I didn't ask about them. I asked about you. Do you still love me?

NAHAR
Without you my life is done! I'd be steamrolled by oblivion. I'm lost without you, you're the very grass of life!

FAIQA
What you were sucking not so long ago wasn't a text or a metaphor. What you were sucking was my breast. So when you talk, talk about that. Not about life, not about grass, not about oblivion.

NAHAR
(*Confused, hogtied by lust, his mind hijacked*) What we were doing is forbidden, absolutely forbidden. Why don't we get married first, and then do it? You become mine, and I become yours. Otherwise, this way...

FAIQA
Now all of a sudden you're permitting and forbidding? Have my breasts become the subject of your new fatwas?

She pulls her breasts out of her bra and hits them forcefully.

This flesh is mine, isn't it? It's not subject to your *fatwas*. If I give it to you, it won't be because of marriage.

NAHAR
Are fatwas forbidden?

FAIQA
Are fatwas your religion, or is the Quran? Is God your God, or is it the speakers who claim they're with God? They forbid you to suck your wife's breast—but themselves they allow everything. That word—"forbidden"—it isn't even your word! Inside you, O Nahar, lives a tiny, ignorant theologian, crammed up against a clueless, stubborn self. That's not you. That's who you need to drive your nails into.

NAHAR
(*Thinking*) Choose fatwas or religion? What kind of talk is that? Aren't fatwas a part of religion? Doesn't God speak through his representatives? What's permitted and forbidden is awfully clear in the text, isn't it?

FAIQA
You're good at asking questions, but your logic is twisted. There is a text, yes—a historical text that transcends time and place. It's made up of verses about specific people and events. Those verses are history, not religion. Right?

NAHAR
Keep going...

FAIQA
These are human matters. The Prophet was human, and his companions were human. Everyone who governed throughout the history of Islam is human, and the theologians are human, too. There's nothing but humans in our religion. If it's human, it can't be absolute. The issue of absoluteness...

NAHAR
Forget all this talk. I want you, okay? I just want you in the permitted way.

FAIQA
Halal is a piece of paper. No? So what stops you from tearing up that halal once you've been with me? Give me a paper that says halal, and you've given me nothing. You're putting my fate in the hands of fool-

ish preachers. You're preventing me from discussing my own fate with you in a serious, human way. My body isn't a subject for a religious contract. It's a private matter. Private between you and me. As if I decide to make a gift of it to you, it means I've decided to liberate my body from a thousand-year-old institution that turns religion into a sword and presses it against our necks.

NAHAR
I don't understand you!

FAIQA
Listen to me. What does religion forbid? Do you know? Tell me.

NAHAR
I know. (*He thinks and thinks.*) I don't know the verses by heart. But there are lots of them. Forbidden things. They're written in the books.

FAIQA
A few things are forbidden in the Quran—just a few. It's the laws built on top of them that are ruining our lives.

NAHAR
Is there a difference?

FAIQA
It's the difference between God and the theologians who speak on His behalf. Between verses and fatwas. God has been slowly pushed out, and scholars have taken His place. The scholars become gods—their words become sacred. But they aren't. They get rich off your money, accumulate wisdom from your ignorance, get free through your slavery and are virtuous on the basis of your abjection. Then they become tools in the hands of rulers, justifying whatever the rulers want. The fatwa replaces religion, and a handful of idiots rule in place of God. The machinery evolves, ignoring constitutions, geography, and history. Soon the faith of mankind is in their hands, not God's. Say they permit something that religion forbids—they simply call the prohibition blasphemy and bless the spilling of blood. Is that our religion?

NAHAR
I don't know...

FAIQA
So now you don't know! Moments ago you wanted to own me with a piece of paper! You wanted to turn my body into a prop for your fake religion.

NAHAR
My religion isn't fake.

FAIQA
Wipe away all the dust, years and years of it, and you'll see where this road is heading.

NAHAR
Do you see the road?

FAIQA
I hate those people. I don't trust them. They've placed our lives under siege with their lies. They draw a circle of prohibition that allows them truth, justice, freedom, and everything else, and they leave us out of it. Their invisible fence, guarded with fatwas, isn't religion. This high stone wall that forbids and excommunicates—it isn't religion. These lies that are the foundation for deprivation, ugliness, fear, beheadings, burning, and death—they are not religion. Religion is a word with values, and love. When humans touch those things, they rot.

NAHAR *doesn't know what to do. He goes to the closet, drags out an old box with his hammer and nails. He secures his own leg to the wall, positions a nail, and hammers it in with calm and steady taps.* FAIQA *remains indifferent.* NAHAR *secures his other leg, positions the nail just above his knee, and taps it in calmly and steadily.* FAIQA *looks at him. Smiles gently. She doesn't seem worried.* NAHAR *secures his backside against the wall, positions a nail above his waist, and fixes it to the wall. A lot of blood is flowing.*

FAIQA *sees that his hands are getting heavier, and his hammer is starting to fall. She holds it up, takes a new nail, positions it over his belly button, and hammers with force. She looks into his eyes—a light appears in them. She sees his mouth, where a flicker of happiness is growing. She takes another nail, positions it over his heart, and starts hammering. Another nail—against his head—and another, and another.*

The OLD MAN *enters and sees* NAHAR *hanging there.*

OLD MAN

(*Indifferently*) You killed a lot of cats this time. The guys at Dog and Cat Pizza will be thrilled. They love the big cats!

FAIQA

(*Speaking like someone who has just gone mad*) They see the wall and learn to worship it—but it's a veil. Their lives pass, and they never see beyond it. They die deprived, hoping for an afterlife without walls. They don't know that the afterlife, too, is surrounded by fences. (*Talking to herself*) No one dares breach the walls. Cursed is the one who tries, and forever mad.

She exposes her chest, lifting it in the air, and rubs it against NAHAR*'s blood-soaked body. She removes her bra, strips naked, and embraces Nahar tightly, crying. The* OLD MAN*, still indifferent, opens the door and exits. A* STREET VENDOR *calls from outside.*

STREET VENDOR

O people of this house! May God curse this house and its inhabitants. Curse those who put my daily bread in your hands.

He opens the door and enters. He sees NAHAR, *hanging there, with* FAIQA *embracing him.*

Two fat cats in one day! Thank you, O God, for your kindness. You've answered my prayer.

He puts NAHAR *in a coffin, then grabs* FAIQA, *wrapping her in plastic from head to toe. Her eyes open and her breath fogs the plastic. Her face disappears behind the vapor. He throws her violently into the coffin and goes.*

ETERNITY

A multimedia play

By Rim Mejdi

Translated by Caline Nasrallah

with additional contributions by Jordan Baum

MA BOHÈME

Je m'en allais, les poings dans mes poches crevées ;
Mon paletot aussi devenait idéal ;
J'allais sous le ciel, Muse ! et j'étais ton féal ;
Oh ! là là ! que d'amours splendides j'ai rêvées !

Mon unique culotte avait un large trou.
- Petit-Poucet rêveur, j'égrenais dans ma course
Des rimes. Mon auberge était à la Grande Ourse.
- Mes étoiles au ciel avaient un doux frou-frou

Et je les écoutais, assis au bord des routes,
Ces bons soirs de septembre où je sentais des gouttes
De rosée à mon front, comme un vin de vigueur ;

Où, rimant au milieu des ombres fantastiques,
Comme des lyres, je tirais les élastiques
De mes souliers blessés, un pied près de mon cœur !

— Arthur Rimbaud

ON *ETERNITY*

We're on a train and the windows are screens. Landscapes roll by on film, reminding us that cinema is just framed rectangular images changing at a steady rate, simulating motion. Is the train "L'eternité" or is it heading toward "L'eternité"? The question doesn't resolve; rather, one possibility is "allée avec" (gone with) the other, or "melée avec" (mixed with) the other.

A train—and perhaps a theater—illustrates the possibility of disappearing into a crowd: it thrusts us into an enclosed space with our neighbors, it also equalizes us by way of our shared practical necessity to be somewhere else. It disrupts our solitary journey from the past to the future with hundreds of other people that crowd into our dream. In Rim Mejdi's *Eternity*, a young man follows Halima, the protagonist of this particular train, into her dream (projected on a screen) only to try to kill himself in it. When she subsequently rebukes him about responsibility, it almost sounds like a traveler telling their neighbor to use their headphones. Pronouns that would seem to distinguish between the people, groups, and ideas on this train are as shifty and restless as the passengers: three officials are the "they" that come to "carry Halima away," but they themselves refer to a "they" who still "might show up." Halima corrects "I'm still thinking" with "I mean, we're still thinking." "L'eternité" herself has cagey pronouns. Introduced by Rimbaud as "elle," we wonder if a person has been "retrouvée" (found), before Rimbaud clarifies that "it" is "L'eternité." The use of ellipses throughout sustains these categorical ellipticalities—circles looking back at themselves.

On the train, groups police others as well as their own members, circles bend but don't break. The men's apprehension of the passengers is both intimate and boundaried: "they" can somehow look at Halima's dreams, but they can't enter them or touch Halima's physical body; they can only touch the apparatus that makes the dreams visible.

Halima, part of the crowd and eventually the audience, is separated internally by sounds and screens, into different voices and bodies, even as she is also separated by the relentless motion of the train, which divides her infinitely as it moves forward. Perhaps this is what creates the restive melancholy we experience on a long train ride. And while the train trafficks in metaphors, Halima's panic also resonates with me on this simple level: it touches the ennui, desperation, boredom, and restless sociality that accompany any train travel.

We're on the train. A man is playing a noisy game on his phone and it's driving everyone crazy. "There's just you, your body, your soul, mixed forever with the noise ... of this train ..." the Elderly Woman tells Halima. Later, the "noise of the train" is "mixed with the roar of the sea," which has been the central image of Halima's dreams of escape. Can we both stay and escape, leave and converge? The sun is "allée avec" the sea or "melée avec" the sea. The phrases, versions of a line from Rimbaud's "L'Eternité," alternate through Mejdi's play. "Allée avec" connotes escape, but also collaboration or convergence, and "melée avec" offers the possibility of both those meanings simultaneously: if you "mix with" someone else, doesn't that mean you, at least partially, disappear?

— Jordan Baum

CHARACTERS

HALIMA	A traveler in her thirties
THE ELDERLY LADY	A traveler in her sixties
THE YOUNG MAN	A traveler in his thirties
THREE OFFICIALS	In their forties
EXTRAS	A few silent travelers

SETTING

May 2021, Marrakesh

NOTE: The characters speak in a colloquial Moroccan dialect. All Arthur Rimbaud poems are spoken in French.

ACT I

SCENE ONE

A train compartment.

HALIMA, *a young woman in her thirties, is reclined in a seat in a train compartment. She is sleeping deeply.*

A MASCULINE VOICE
Wake up. It's time for you to wake up.

Assez vu. La vision s'est rencontrée à tous les airs.
Assez eu. Rumeurs des villes, le soir, et au soleil, et toujours.
Assez connu. Les arrêts de la vie. —O rumeurs et Visions !
Départ dans l'affection et le bruit neufs ![1]

HALIMA *wakes up suddenly, as if from a nightmare.*

HALIMA
What was that?

HALIMA *looks around in astonishment. She sees the other passengers, asleep, and an old lady who's awake.* HALIMA *gets up and takes a few steps, exploring the compartment.*

Two screens behind HALIMA *are illuminated, first one, then the other. As if through a pair of train windows, we see waiting trains give way to a deserted landscape.* HALIMA *looks at the screens, stunned, then approaches them and touches one.*

HALIMA *goes back to her seat.*

AN INNER VOICE
What am I doing here? How did I get here?

---

1 "Départ" by Arthur Rimbaud, *Illuminations*

HALIMA
I don't understand. Where am I?

THE ELDERLY LADY
(*Whispering*) Are you okay, my child?

HALIMA
No, I was asleep, someone woke me up, I found myself here…

THE ELDERLY LADY *gets up and approaches* HALIMA.

THE ELDERLY LADY
(*Whispering*) I'll tell you a secret to calm you down, I found myself here, too, in the same way. I don't know how it happened, I don't remember, but you shouldn't say it. You have to pretend to know, that's what I'm doing, otherwise we don't know what might happen…

HALIMA
What do you mean? Have you been here for a while? What might happen to us?

THE ELDERLY LADY
(*Whispering*) I don't remember how much time it's been, it feels like a while, but I can't tell how long… but don't wonder why, don't think about it. Just pretend, you'll get used to it… and if you get bored, sleep!

HALIMA
Otherwise what happens? If I do wonder? Is there anyone I can ask?

THE ELDERLY LADY
If you ask, they'll take you from here, and only God knows where they'll take you.

HALIMA
What do you mean? Who are they?

THE ELDERLY LADY
I don't know, but they show up every time someone has a fit and

starts screaming. They come and take the person. We don't even know how they come, or how they know what is happening. They come down and carry the person away.

HALIMA
So there are other people who already asked before me? What do the other passengers think?

THE ELDERLY LADY
Everyone prefers to keep quiet so they can stay on the train, there are rumors swirling...

HALIMA
What rumors?

THE ELDERLY LADY
That the people who have fits, they throw them to the wild beasts outside, they throw them off the moving train...

HALIMA *puts her head back on the seat and takes a breath. She looks out the window at the landscapes rolling past.*

AN INNER VOICE
What am I doing here? Where is this train even headed? I need to ask at the next stop.

HALIMA
Ma'am, I'm going to have to bother you again. How long until the next stop?

THE ELDERLY LADY
My child, you ask a lot of questions and you're going to drag me into your trouble. Knowing won't get you anywhere. You can't get off unless they choose you. They're the ones who decide the fate of who stays and who leaves.

HALIMA
And if I want to leave?

THE ELDERLY LADY

Want to? What does that mean? I've never heard this verb in my life. What language are you speaking?

HALIMA

What? I don't understand what's going on!

THE ELDERLY LADY

My child, this is how people start getting into fits, and how they get thrown to the wolves ...take it easy, don't ask useless questions.

HALIMA

Fine, this is my last question. Where is the train headed? I mean, its final destination?

THE ELDERLY LADY

Now you're asking me about the unknown ...None of us knows. The important thing is to stay on board, not to ask too many questions, and one day we will reach our destination, inshallah.

HALIMA *turns to the other* PASSENGERS.

HALIMA

Please, sir, do you know where we are going?

The PASSENGER *does not answer. He just closes his eyes.*

HALIMA *turns to some other* PASSENGERS. *Some of them are asleep; others seem absent.*

HALIMA

(*Having a fit*) What kind of madness is this? Are you all crazy ...all of you? Traveling on a train you don't even know the destination of, pretending like nothing's going on ...I can't pretend like you! Where are we going?! In what direction? I want to get off this damn train—right now.

ANONYMOUS OFFICIALS *descend on the compartment and carry* HALIMA *away.*

ACT II

SCENE ONE

Smoking Section.

HALIMA *finds herself in another compartment on the same train. It is a large cage, made from lasers, that is open from the front. A sign is hung up in the middle of the cage. It says:* SMOKING SECTION.

A nocturnal landscape appears on the screens. The moon alone is shining through the darkness of the night. HALIMA *is in a seat. Three* ANONYMOUS OFFICIALS *surround her.*

OFFICIAL ONE
Sleep well?

OFFICIAL TWO
You hungry?

OFFICIAL THREE
Thirsty?

HALIMA
Where am I?

OFFICIAL TWO
Here we go again, back to the questions. Mrs. Halima, or should I call you Miss? I hope it's not offensive that I call you Miss? You seem to never know where you are. You've got a real memory problem!

HALIMA
How do you know my name?

OFFICIAL ONE
You told us what it was, did you forget that too? A real memory problem.

The three of them suddenly fall silent. They walk

around HALIMA, *crossing and re-crossing the stage. Then they form a circle with* HALIMA *at the center. They walk counterclockwise.*

HALIMA *is just watching their choreography.*

OFFICIAL THREE
What do we do in this case?
Don't worry, we'll take care of it.

OFFICIAL THREE *exits stage left. The other two* OFFICIALS *are staring at* HALIMA.

OFFICIAL ONE
Are you sure you're not hungry?

HALIMA
Ever since I woke up here, I haven't felt hungry or thirsty ... What am I doing here? Who brought me here?

OFFICIAL TWO
You came of your own free will. I'm sure you don't remember that. Look in your pockets, you'll find the ticket.

The OFFICIALS *light their cigarettes at the same time.* HALIMA *coughs.*

HALIMA *checks her pockets. She finds a ticket and examines it.*

HALIMA
There's no destination on this ticket. It can't be, this isn't mine.

OFFICIAL THREE
Your name is on it. You used your bank card to buy it.

HALIMA *looks at the ticket again.*

HALIMA
(*Astonished*) That's true!

OFFICIAL THREE re-enters stage right in a doctor's lab coat, carrying a small satchel.

OFFICIAL TWO
A real memory problem!

OFFICIAL THREE
Hello, ma'am, they told me you were suffering from a memory problem. I'm going to have to ask you to relax while I examine you.

HALIMA
You're not a doctor, you're with them, you just left earlier…

OFFICIAL TWO
No, Halima, he's a doctor…Let him do his job…

HALIMA
Is this a joke? No, that's not a doctor!

OFFICIAL ONE
It's true that he looks like our colleague. But it's not him…

OFFICIAL TWO
There is an uncanny resemblance. We've always said so ourselves!

OFFICIAL THREE
Come on, miss, open your mouth and say ahhh!

HALIMA refuses to engage. She looks at them, indifferent.

OFFICIAL TWO
Come on, Halima, don't be stubborn!

OFFICIAL THREE forcefully opens HALIMA's mouth.

OFFICIAL THREE
Very good.

OFFICIAL THREE *examines* HALIMA *with a stethoscope.*

OFFICIAL ONE

Now tell me, how did you get here? What's the last thing you remember?

He takes out a small recorder.

HALIMA

I don't know, I don't remember anything…the last thing I remember is falling asleep in my own bed…

OFFICIAL TWO

Excellent, you're doing great…you don't remember waking up? Packing your bag? Heading to the station and buying the train ticket?

HALIMA

No, absolutely not, none of that!

OFFICIAL TWO

But that is what really happened! You got up earlier than usual, snuck out of your house, and bought a train ticket!

HALIMA

How do you know all this?

OFFICIAL THREE

We know. We know everything. That's it.

HALIMA

How?

OFFICIAL THREE

It doesn't matter how…We know you well, but you don't know us. It's simple, we know everything, we know everyone…

HALIMA

…and yet I've never seen you before. Are you a jinn? To know everything?

OFFICIAL THREE

These questions are useless. Let's continue.

OFFICIAL ONE

So, you came here of your own free will. When the agent at the window asked you where you were going, what did you say?

HALIMA

What? I didn't see anyone ...if what you say is true, how did I get on a train with no destination? That's impossible ...

OFFICIAL ONE

It is possible. When he asked you: What is your destination, ma'am? You said: I don't know, anywhere but here.

HALIMA

I never said that. That's not true. You're driving me crazy! There is no train that runs without a destination!

OFFICIAL TWO

Yes, there is. The proof is that you're on one right now, and you boarded of your own free will. Even if you can't remember, we do!

THE OTHER TWO OFFICIALS

(*Together*) Yes, we remember!

HALIMA

I want to get off at the next stop. What's the next stop?

The OFFICIALS *are quiet.*

HALIMA

I asked you: what's the next stop? There must be a next stop!

OFFICIAL THREE

This is beyond our capabilities ...

OFFICIAL ONE

We don't know.

OFFICIAL TWO
This ... we don't know ...

HALIMA
Take me to the person who does!

THE THREE OFFICIALS
(*Together*) Wait for them here, they might show up ... and they might not ...

HALIMA
How long do I wait?

SCENE TWO

HALIMA sleeps in her seat, alone in a new compartment.

On the screens, images of a red desert and a figure approaching the camera. We see that it's HALIMA, running, out of breath. We hear her in voice-over.

HALIMA

I've finally managed to escape. Now I can go wherever I want to, I'm free from that damn train. A train without a destination!

HALIMA sleeps. On the screen behind her, she is walking calmly.

HALIMA

I'm free from those stupid, silent passengers, pretending to know where they're going...I won't be like them. I'll go where I want to, I know where to go...but where am I going? I can decide myself.

On the screen, THE ELDERLY LADY appears.

THE ELDERLY LADY

Wait, my child, I don't have the energy to run all the way up to you.

HALIMA

What are you doing here, ma'am?

THE ELDERLY LADY

I'm coming with you. Isn't that obvious?

HALIMA

Why would you do that? You're an old lady, you should have stayed on the train!

THE ELDERLY LADY

I won't let you run through the desert alone like a wild beast! I'm coming with you! Do you at least know where you're going?

HALIMA
Yes ... (*A pause*)
I'm going ...west, to where the sun sets ...

HALIMA *walks and* THE ELDERLY LADY *struggles to catch up with her.* HALIMA *feels she has to help her keep walking.*

The women walk together. The sun sinks.

The stage lights blink out.

SCENE THREE

The stage lights blink on.

HALIMA *sleeps.*

On one screen, HALIMA *is moving away from us, crossing the sand with* THE ELDERLY LADY.

On the other, HALIMA *is moving towards us, approaching the sea on a wild beach, holding* THE ELDERLY LADY*'s hand.*

HALIMA
(*Voice-over, whispering*) *L'éternité, c'est la mer mêlée avec le soleil.*

THE ELDERLY LADY
No, we didn't find it. You didn't find it.

HALIMA
Excuse me, what?

THE ELDERLY LADY
You heard me. You haven't found anything. This isn't eternity! It's just the sea and sun. They don't meet!

HALIMA, *asleep on the compartment seat, is woken up from her dream by a* YOUNG MAN *of* HALIMA*'s age entering.*

HALIMA
Who are you??

THE YOUNG MAN
You haven't found anything. This isn't eternity. It's just the sea and sun. They don't meet.

HALIMA
Who are you?

THE YOUNG MAN
I don't know…All I know is that I'm running away from them…

HALIMA
What's your name then, fugitive?

THE YOUNG MAN
I don't know…with time, I forgot…this damn train makes you forget everything.

HALIMA
You even forgot your own name? That can't be!

THE YOUNG MAN
It was on the tip of my tongue, but whenever I tried to remember, they'd descend on me and grab me. So I gave up trying…and I forgot.

HALIMA *gets up and approaches* THE YOUNG MAN.

HALIMA
Where do we escape to?

THE YOUNG MAN
I don't know, anywhere…but they're everywhere, wherever you go. I run away, they find me. Even in the dreams I ran away in…

HALIMA
What? They follow you in a dream?

THE YOUNG MAN *lies down on the floor and stares up in contemplation.*

THE YOUNG MAN
No, they don't have that ability…but I don't dream anymore…when I sleep, it's like I'm in a deep, dark, bottomless valley. I wish I had nightmares, even—anything…but all images, all dreams disappeared little by little, the more time passed on this damn train.

HALIMA
Do you know how much time has passed?

THE YOUNG MAN
No ...it feels like forever, but I could have just gotten here yesterday.

HALIMA *lies down, not far from him.*

HALIMA
How come I dream, then?

THE YOUNG MAN
I don't know, maybe because you're a newcomer ...or maybe you're stronger.

THE YOUNG MAN *gets up.*

THE YOUNG MAN
Enough talk. I have to hide ...it was nice to meet you.

THE YOUNG MAN *is about to leave.* HALIMA *stops him.*

HALIMA
I know a hiding place where they won't find you.

THE YOUNG MAN *turns to her eagerly.*

THE YOUNG MAN
Where? ...Quick, please!

HALIMA
In my dream ...unlike you, I can still dream. They won't be able to find you there ... come here.

THE YOUNG MAN *walks to where* HALIMA *is and lies down next to her.*

HALIMA
Close your eyes.

Behind them the two screens: on one, we see a live-feed from the corner of the ceiling. It's an overhead shot showing HALIMA *and* THE YOUNG

MAN *lying on their backs. On the other, we see a seascape.*

HALIMA

We're in the sea...the beach is beautiful, despite how gloomy it looks...the sun goes down and the sea...it's calling us to purify ourselves.

HALIMA *puts her hand on* THE YOUNG MAN's *head. He immediately falls asleep, as if he's being hypnotized.*

The lights go out, and the screens stay on.

On the screen, we see THE YOUNG MAN *walking ahead, filmed from behind. He walks toward the sea and throws himself in it.*

On the other screen, THE YOUNG MAN *appears filmed from the front, holding his breath before diving underwater.* HALIMA *appears. She follows* THE YOUNG MAN *and catches him, pulling him out of the water toward the shore.*

HALIMA *lays* THE YOUNG MAN *down and administers CPR.*

The screens go off.

Onstage, THE YOUNG MAN *is trying to breathe and spitting out water. He seems shaken, choked. He gasps for air and has a panic attack.*

THE YOUNG MAN

What am I doing here? Let me go. You should have just let me drown.

HALIMA

Can't do that. You were in my dream, your life is my responsibility... go into someone else's dream and kill yourself if you want to.

THE YOUNG MAN gets up. He is facing HALIMA. HALIMA squares herself.

THE YOUNG MAN
It's my life!

HALIMA
It's my dream!

THE YOUNG MAN
What's a dream compared to life?!

HALIMA
What's a life without dreams?!

Desperate, THE YOUNG MAN turns away from her.

THE YOUNG MAN
I thought you'd help me, that you understood me. But these are my own delusions…I will never enter anyone's dream again. I don't want dreams—not mine, not anyone else's…I just want to go away, far away. To really leave with my body, my senses, not to resort to fleeting dreams only to return to square one when they end. To this damn train.

HALIMA
Do what you want. Right now, I don't have anything but my dreams to hide in. Everything you're saying is just out of jealousy and envy… because you've lost your own dreams. I'm not going to care about your despair. Take it far away and go. I'll stay in this prison of mine until I know what to do, or until I figure out what the next stop is.

THE YOUNG MAN laughs at her mockingly.

THE YOUNG MAN
You think you're going to figure it out?

HALIMA
I know I will.

THE YOUNG MAN
How bold!

We can hear voices approaching.

THE YOUNG MAN
They're coming! What do I do? Where do I hide?

HALIMA *and* THE YOUNG MAN *panic.*

HALIMA
In my dream, they won't find you ...but I'm warning you, don't do anything reckless ...I don't want a corpse in my dreams that I can't get rid of.

HALIMA *lies down on the floor.* THE YOUNG MAN *lies down behind her. They close their eyes.*

The three OFFICIALS *enter.*

SCENE FOUR

The OFFICIALS *enter and explore the compartment. They look at the screens, on which* HALIMA *and* THE YOUNG MAN *can be seen from behind, contemplating the sea.*

OFFICIAL TWO
She's asleep ... she must have given up, like the others.

OFFICIAL ONE
How tiring and curious this one is!

OFFICIAL THREE
What annoys me about her is her faith—it's why she's so stubborn.

OFFICIAL TWO
It will fade, don't worry. It will all fade ...we ourselves faded.

OFFICIAL TWO *sits on the floor, visibly sad.*

OFFICIAL THREE
What's wrong, buddy? Did you forget that we're not them?

OFFICIAL TWO
I'm tired of chasing them, I'm tired of imprisoning them, I'm tired of pretending that I know more than them and that I have the answers to their questions. I'm tired of pretending to be keeping the answers from them ...I'm tired of this damn train, how long will it go on like this, without slowing down or speeding up? It hasn't changed its pace!

OFFICIAL ONE
Look, she's dreaming of a young man! Ha ha ha, he must be her lover.

The three OFFICIALS *look at the screen, where* HALIMA *and* THE YOUNG MAN *are contemplating the sea, holding each other.*

HALIMA
(*Onstage, whispering*) We did it! They don't suspect a thing.

OFFICIAL TWO
She's so lucky, still dreaming, and about love, too...I've forgotten the taste of love. I only remember that it fills every atom in our bodies. But without actually feeling it, it's just an abstract idea...the truth is that I've completely forgotten what it feels like. It's just letters, a sound.

The other two OFFICIALS *look at their colleague and move to a far corner.*

OFFICIAL ONE
I think he's starting to lose his mind. What do we do?

OFFICIAL THREE
It'll pass, I'm sure.

OFFICIAL ONE
And if it continues? He's empathizing, even identifying with them. In my opinion we should report and release him.

OFFICIAL THREE
Let's give him some time. Don't rush.

OFFICIAL ONE
What if his words get to us? What if we're contaminated with his craziness? Then we'd all be thrown to the wild beasts.

OFFICIAL THREE *thinks about this, looking at his colleague.*

OFFICIAL TWO *gets up and approaches the image of* HALIMA *and* THE YOUNG MAN. *He touches the screen.*

OFFICIAL TWO
How beautiful Halima is... even the way she sits, the way her back looks... I wish I could enter her dream and sit there, where that man is.

OFFICIAL ONE *and* OFFICIAL THREE *look at each other and approach* OFFICIAL TWO.

OFFICIAL ONE

Come on, let's continue our rounds. She's asleep, we'll talk to her when she wakes up.

OFFICIAL THREE

Yes, let's go. It's no use being here.

OFFICIAL TWO

Leave me here, I just want to watch her dream. It's been a long time since I had a dream.

His colleagues drag him away, as if he were a prisoner.

THE ELDERLY LADY *enters.*

SCENE FIVE

THE ELDERLY LADY *looks at* HALIMA *and* THE YOUNG MAN, *who are lying down and dreaming.*

THE ELDERLY LADY
Elle est retrouvée.
Quoi ? - L'Éternité.
C'est la mer allée
Avec le soleil.[2]

Her voice wakes HALIMA. HALIMA *looks at* THE YOUNG MAN, *asleep beside her, then turns to* THE ELDERLY LADY.

HALIMA
Why do you follow me everywhere I go?

THE ELDERLY LADY
I will never leave you. I'll follow you everywhere until you return to the compartment. That's where you should be ...nowhere else ...

HALIMA
Leave me alone. I want to find my way home. Enough already!

THE ELDERLY LADY
The compartment is your home ...or have you forgotten?

HALIMA
No, no!

THE ELDERLY LADY
Well, where do you live then?

HALIMA
I don't know, I don't know anymore. That's the problem.

2 "The Song of the Highest Tower" by Arthur Rimbaud, *Fêtes de la Patience*

THE ELDERLY LADY

Do you have any other memories? Places, people, moments?

HALIMA *is quiet.*

THE ELDERLY LADY

Come on, try!

HALIMA

I can't, everything in me is empty, it's all empty. Like nothing existed before!

THE ELDERLY LADY

I'll tell you a secret. It's a secret that everyone discovers at some point, that no one dares say out loud: there's no point in trying to remember ...because there's nothing for us to remember ... there was nothing before the train. There's just you, your body, your soul, blended forever with this noise and forward motion ...And until you accept it you'll be living in hell.

HALIMA

But why do I get the feeling that there's something I need to remember? Something stashed away deep inside me. It's like there's a door that hides the truth, a door I don't have the key to.

THE ELDERLY LADY

It's the illusion your brain has created to resist, to resist the ones who took you, to resist the hostility of the passengers, to resist the unknown, to resist the fact that we don't even know the destination of this damn train, where it's taking us! I went through the same thing when I was your age. An old lady revealed the truth to me then, my truth, your truth ...a truth at once so simple and so difficult to grasp.

HALIMA

I want to die. I can't do this anymore; I don't want to resist. Let this whole train crash with all its stupid passengers. I don't care. I want to go far, far away. I want to escape. That's what I want! To escape and keep running until my breath stops, until my heart explodes, anything but stay on this train! I'll run away with this young man. He's like me. He understands me, he longs to break free.

THE ELDERLY LADY

Do you think that if you leave, you'll be better off? Or that love will save you? That's just another illusion ... I'm telling you, you'll never be better off elsewhere because this is your place, here, on this train. Why don't you be patient? Maybe you'll find out one day where the train is headed, what its destination is. Why say the choice is leaving or dying? You're being melodramatic!

HALIMA

Because I'm young and full of life. I want to understand, I don't want to pretend. You, you're old, resigned, you want to pretend! I'm not like you. I have to go!

THE ELDERLY LADY

Love is doomed to disappear. It's another illusion. You'll regret it later, when it's too late.

HALIMA

What are you saying? Who's talking about love?

HALIMA *turns away, angry.*

THE ELDERLY LADY

You said you wanted to run away with the young man.

HALIMA

Just because we both long to be free. We want to leave and would rather die than fail. But you don't understand these things. Your mind is rigid. Your heart is dead. Yes, they killed your heart, and you didn't mind—you gave in. But I'm not like you. We're not like you. And now, ma'am, leave me alone. Please.

THE ELDERLY LADY

Fine. And what will you do? Do you have an escape plan? Have you found a way out?

HALIMA *is silent for a moment.*

HALIMA
I'm still thinking. I mean, we're still thinking. For now, I'm staying here with this young man—or rather, he's going to stay hidden in my dream until we figure something out.

HALIMA *returns to her place beside* THE YOUNG MAN, *who is still asleep.*

On the screen, we see them from above, lying down. THE YOUNG MAN*'s eyes are closed.* HALIMA *is awake.*

THE ELDERLY LADY
What a brave plan, a shrewd plan: sleeping and hiding in a dream. Really, I want to congratulate you on your cleverness, Halima.

HALIMA
This has nothing to do with you, ma'am. Leave me alone now, please. I do what I want. I am free.

THE ELDERLY LADY
You've been thinking of no one but yourself from the beginning! Me, me, me ...what about the other passengers? What about the train? Are you going to leave your seat vacant? What if everyone else's survival depends on your being here? What then? What if this is way bigger than you? What if you absolutely had to be here, what if here is your place? What then? You don't care about anyone but yourself—leaving, leaving! Aren't you afraid you'll regret it?

HALIMA
I'm afraid of wasting my life here, my meaningless life, my life ...

THE YOUNG MAN
(Screaming, in voice-over) Oisive jeunesse, à toute asservie, par délicatesse, j'ai perdu ma vie !

HALIMA
I'm afraid of losing my mind, and of shouting these words when I'm old! Why are you so anxious to convince me? It's those officials,

they've sent you, haven't they? To talk me out of leaving, to talk me out of being free?

THE ELDERLY LADY

Poor girl, you haven't understood a thing. What I'm doing here is bigger than you, bigger than those officials, even bigger than me, than all of our lives combined... but you won't understand this right now. You'll only understand when it's too late.

HALIMA

But this is exactly what I want—to understand. What is there to understand? Tell me, is there anything to understand?

THE ELDERLY LADY

Let me make a deal with you. You're looking for eternity? You'll get it, if you stay in the compartment and finish the journey ...eternity will be given to you—a happy, prosperous, and peaceful eternity. You'll never grow old like me. What do you think?

HALIMA

What do I get out of all this? This is hell! What's the meaning behind it all?

HALIMA *sits down and says nothing for a while. She watches herself and* THE YOUNG MAN *on the screen behind her, then looks at* THE ELDERLY LADY.

HALIMA

What do I get out of all this? What use is eternity to me?

THE ELDERLY LADY

Maybe then you'll find out where this damn train, as you call it, is going... Think about it... maybe that's why you got on board in the first place. You'll finally understand!

HALIMA

I'm not a child, don't mess with me.

THE ELDERLY LADY

I'm telling you, there is something hidden that you must know, that you will not know unless you complete your journey on this train. Stay here now. You'll discover the secret later, and with it, eternity.

HALIMA *lies down and closes her eyes. She takes* THE YOUNG MAN*'s hand. He is asleep. Behind her, on the screen, we see a train advancing through the night in a desert landscape. But there's something wrong with the images; they don't seem real.*

A MASCULINE VOICE

Sleep now, sleep ...but you are condemned to wake up ...

THE ELDERLY LADY *leaves.*

L'hiver, nous irons dans un petit wagon rose
Avec des coussins bleus.
Nous serons bien. Un nid de baisers fous repose
Dans chaque coin moelleux.
Tu fermeras l'œil, pour ne point voir, par la glace,
Grimacer les ombres des soirs,
Ces monstruosités hargneuses, populace
De démons noirs et de loups noirs.
Puis tu te sentiras la joue égratignée...
Un petit baiser, comme une folle araignée,
Te courra par le cou...
Et tu me diras : "Cherche !", en inclinant la tête,
- Et nous prendrons du temps à trouver cette bête
Qui voyage beaucoup...[3]

3 "Rêvé pour l'hiver" by Arthur Rimbaud, *En Wagon*, October 7, 1870.

ACT III

SCENE ONE

Smoking Section.

HALIMA *gets up and notices that* THE YOUNG MAN *is gone. The screens are off. She takes a few steps.*

Suddenly he appears.

HALIMA
Where did you go?

THE YOUNG MAN
I didn't want to wake you. I went looking, trying to see if there's a way out…but we have to be careful. They're alert.

HALIMA
Okay.

THE YOUNG MAN
Why so indifferent? I thought you'd be jumping for joy. I'm telling you we're about to be free!

HALIMA
By leaving?

THE YOUNG MAN
Yes, come on, trust me. We'll get off this cursed train together. I promise!

HALIMA
Is leaving the only solution?

THE YOUNG MAN
What's with you? What happened? You won't let me die, now you won't let me leave. Yes, leaving is the best solution, let's go far away from here.

HALIMA
Far away where?

THE YOUNG MAN

I don't know. Away. To our own path, where life is.

HALIMA

Do you know a place other than this place? I don't remember anywhere else. I don't know anywhere else. There is no other place for me than here. Do you have somewhere that's yours, other than here?

THE YOUNG MAN

What's gotten into you? You've changed your tune!

HALIMA

Answer me. Where is your path? Where is your home? Where is the place you call yours? Your own?

THE YOUNG MAN

I don't know. All I know is that I need to get out of here. I have no other choice. I need to leave, or else…

HALIMA

Or else what?

THE YOUNG MAN

(*Shouting*) Or else, madness or death. A slow death. A pointless death. No.

HALIMA *takes a few steps and then sits down.*

HALIMA

I don't know anywhere that's not here. My seat is in the compartment. I don't remember any other place. I'd rather that than be a stranger somewhere else.

THE YOUNG MAN

What happened, why'd you turn on me? You're being delusional! We're strangers here already. What do we have here? We can't even decide where to go, what stop to get off at…that decision's not ours to make. We can't make any decisions, can't have any opinions. How much more of a stranger can one be?

HALIMA

You're not seeing things clearly. We do have a decision to make—we could decide to stay, to keep going until the train makes it to its destination. We could keep asking and asking and searching until we find the answer. Leaving is easy. Leaving is the real surrender.

THE YOUNG MAN

Surrender is staying where death and stagnation reign. They've corrupted you; they've brainwashed you with empty ideas.

HALIMA

You're the one living in an illusion. The illusion of your whim. You follow these whims, thinking they're your soul.

THE YOUNG MAN

They showed you a false picture of things. Come with me, save your own skin. No one else will care about you, don't trust anyone. Save yourself first. Think of your freedom, your destiny.

HALIMA

I don't want to save my own skin. Freedom is understanding where I'm headed. It's understanding where this train is going. Freedom is reaching eternity.

THE YOUNG MAN

That's it, your mind has been corrupted! What eternity are you talking about? Who filled your brain with all this nonsense? There is no eternity. We just have to stay vigilant so they don't get us. So we can get free. That's why we have to leave. Freedom is leaving.

HALIMA

You're just talking about an escape. Isn't that it? Running away from everything? You're cynical and nihilistic. You only care about yourself. But you run from yourself too!

THE YOUNG MAN

That's not true! (*Shouting*) I'm running from injustice and absurdity, not from myself!

HALIMA
What's your name, then?

THE YOUNG MAN *goes quiet.*

THE YOUNG MAN
What do you mean?

HALIMA
I said, what's your name?

THE YOUNG MAN
I don't remember!

HALIMA
See? You think you can convince me when you don't even remember your name?

THE YOUNG MAN
Shame on you. You know they're the ones who made me forget my name.

HALIMA
I don't know that. How come I can remember my name then? Why? It's easy to blame them for everything. It's too easy. If you don't remember your name or where you come from or where your place is—that's your problem. Take a little responsibility instead of whining like a child and threatening to leave.

THE YOUNG MAN
No, they are the reason. They took everything from me. I have to leave to stop them from taking more. They'll take everything from you, too. You're still new here. You'll see. Mark my words. Do whatever you want. I'm leaving.

HALIMA
Then leave. What are you waiting for? You want me to beg you to stay? To kiss you and hug you and tell you how important and precious you are, that your staying is a matter of life or death? That your being here is absolutely necessary? That your absence will be felt?

Go! If you don't want to resist, that's your business. But please don't change the facts. Don't delude yourself and call escaping a virtue or any kind of real resistance.

THE YOUNG MAN

Don't be cruel. Not everyone has your strength and faith.
I won't forget you.

HALIMA

I already forgot you!

THE YOUNG MAN *leaves.*

SCENE TWO

OFFICIAL ONE and OFFICIAL THREE reappear. HALIMA is seated and seems to have been waiting for them.

OFFICIAL ONE
So? Did you get some rest?

HALIMA
Yes. Where is the old lady?

OFFICIAL THREE
She decided to go, but she gave us a message for you: she left you her seat.

HALIMA gets up and looks at them sternly.

HALIMA
I want to go back to my compartment now.

OFFICIAL ONE
What happened, miss? Do you finally remember how you got here?

HALIMA
Yes, I remember. I packed my suitcase and wanted to get on the train. I remember the agent at the station and that the train had no destination, and still I wanted to get on board. It happened because I wanted it, and I must go back.

OFFICIAL THREE
Why are you so desperate to go back all of a sudden?

HALIMA is silent for a while.

HALIMA
I don't remember. But I'm sure that if I go back to the compartment I will. I know that it's very important, that it's bigger than my own life and desires or frustrations. It's bigger even than my existence and my

death. And knowing that is enough to make me want to go back. That was what I wanted from the start, from the moment I packed my bag and bought the ticket ... Take me back, kill me even, but take my body back to my compartment.

Where is your friend?

Silently, the OFFICIALS *glance at each other.*

OFFICIAL ONE
We don't know.

They lead her off.

SCENE THREE

Train compartment/a theater.

HALIMA *appears at the front of the house. She looks at the audience, and then sits with them, in the first row. Next to her is* THE ELDERLY LADY*'s seat, empty.* HALIMA *looks serene. Before her, on stage, the two screens: on one, an unfolding landscape, as if from a train window. On the other, a sun setting over the wild beach. In the second video, we see* HALIMA *from behind, contemplating the sea,* THE ELDERLY LADY *beside her. The noise of the train blends with the roar of the sea. As* HALIMA *contemplates herself and the seascape on the screen,* THE ELDERLY LADY*'s voice fills the space.*

THE ELDERLY LADY
(Voice-over) Elle est retrouvée.
Quoi ? - L'Éternité.
C'est la mer allée
Avec le soleil.
Âme sentinelle,
Murmurons l'aveu
De la nuit si nulle
Et du jour en feu.
Des humains suffrages,
Des communs élans
Là tu te dégages
Et voles selon.
Puisque de vous seules,
Braises de satin,
Le Devoir s'exhale
Sans qu'on dise : enfin.
Là pas d'espérance,

Nul orietur.
Science avec patience,
Le supplice est sûr.
Elle est retrouvée.
Quoi ? - L'Éternité.
C'est la mer allée
Avec le soleil.[4]

4 "L'éternité" by Arthur Rimbaud, *Derniers Vers*, May 1872.

LEFT OUT GONE BAD

by Yasser Abu Shaqra

translated anonymously

with additional contributions by Agnes Borinsky

ON *LEFT OUT GONE BAD*

"It's impossible to have a conversation in this house."

With *Left Out Gone Bad*, Yasser Abu Shaqra has written a play as compact and brutal as a knot. It posits as its problem and its wound the impossibility of having conversations. A family with no last name has migrated from Syria to an unnamed country in Europe. The move has stripped them all of some measure of identity—the parents are referred to only as "Father" and "Mother"—but even more than that it has stripped them of the ability to speak to one another.

Abu Shaqra told me that the trickiest parts of this play to translate are the insults. When does calling someone an "asshole" cross a line? When is it tender, funny? How do you calibrate all the social meanings in English of "dick," "punk," or "fucker"? Here it's not just the translator's problem, but the problem of the play. How do people who love each other proceed when their realities have become mutually untranslatable? When the social meaning of a life can no longer be deciphered by all the people trying to live it?

There's a certain kind of play in which each character has a worldview to espouse. The playwright's job is to position, complicate, and ironize. To fluff the audience's sense of its own capacity for empathy. It's the dramaturgical equivalent of what journalist Alex V. Green has called the "Having Conversations Industrial Complex." Green means the loose constellation of professional speakers, consultants, organizations, politicians, and public personalities who are paid to generate a "conversation" that may not have any tangible result. In these conversations, much is said, little is dared. One feels a mounting panic that everything that matters has been lost in translation.

In *Left Out Gone Bad*, the violence happens offstage. The violence happens in language. I swing the knot of this play over my head and it becomes clear how much damage it could do. The scope of the tragedy is global—and yet it all unfolds through the act of speaking. Words miss, and that's what's so devastating. The bedrock of love is a sense that when I speak, you hear me. My words land somewhere. In *Left Out Gone Bad*, characters listen for the moment when their words will land, only to realize that their words are instead falling endlessly into a void. Love isn't doing what love does. What happened? Maybe their words will never land, will plummet, untranslated and untranslatable.

When conversation becomes impossible, where does love go? As the father says, "Of course they're right. And I'm right. And you're right. And Wafi and Samar are right. But why are we all in so much pain?"

– Agnes Borinsky

CHARACTERS

FATHER 55 years old.

MOTHER 50 years old.

SAMAR Their daughter, 28 years old. She has lived in Europe for three years.

WAFI Their son, 16 years old. He has lived in Europe for three years.

OBEIDA Their paternal aunt, 48 years old. She has lived in Europe for three and a half years.

SAAD Samar's boyfriend, later her husband, 25 years old. He has lived in Europe for three and a half years.

ACT I

A few days after the parents have arrived. Kitchen. FATHER *and* WAFI *sit at the table.* SAMAR *stands nearby with* SAAD. SAAD*'s outfit is baggy. The* MOTHER *sits on a couch, holding a cellphone. Though the kitchen extends past what we can see, there appears to be a pot boiling on the stove.*

FATHER
It feels like a window's open.

WAFI
No, Dad. Everything's shut. We can barely breathe in here.

SAMAR
Every day since you got here we've been afraid to air out the apartment.

MOTHER
We opened a window and almost froze to death.

SAAD
Well, this is spring. You should see winter.

FATHER
Oh, please. Give me cold weather as long as the heating works. Much better than nice weather and scrambling to meet basic needs.

WAFI
God! Talk about basic needs. The smell of Imm[1] el-Hassan's cooking...You should have come sooner.

MOTHER
Like I had a choice.

FATHER
All we wanted was to get out after Hassan was killed. Then they decide to arrest Muwafak just as we're leaving. May God set him free.

---

1 Individuals are customarily nicknamed *Abu* (father of) or *Imm* (mother of) with the name of their first male child. In this case, the father is nicknamed Abu el-Hassan and the mother Imm el-Hassan after their eldest son, Hassan.

SAMAR

(*To* SAAD) Literally the day after our brother was arrested they ordered us out…So we scrambled to borrow money from everyone we knew and ran.

WAFI

Let's play cards. Wanna play, Abu el-Hassan?

SAAD

I'd be down to play.

SAAD *joins them at the table.*

FATHER

(*After a brief silence*) No thanks. Not in the mood.

MOTHER

Your Aunt Obeida just texted. She's on her way.

SAMAR

On her way? What happened?

FATHER

What do you mean, what happened?

SAMAR

She and her husband argue sometimes. But to come all the way out here?

WAFI

Her husband's a dick.

FATHER

You're a dick.

WAFI

Wow, Abu el-Hassan. Okay. (*He laughs.*) I swear, meeting you at the airport it seemed like you were back from a vacation. A whole welcoming committee! Who gets that kind of welcome, showing up for life in a new country?

MOTHER
I'm grateful. So many sweet people.

FATHER
It was a close call. If you'd turned eighteen we wouldn't have been eligible for Family Reunification anymore.

SAMAR
(*To* SAAD) It was awful. I was just sitting there thinking that my parents might be there, and we could be here, and that would just be it. We'd never see each other again.

MOTHER
No, dear, hopefully it's over. Now we're together things will be easier.

SAMAR
I swear, Mom, we went through hell to get you here.

FATHER
The whole process was miserable—hell for us, too.

MOTHER
I was sure it wouldn't work. I used to pray to God every night: Please, don't take all four of my children. I never did anything to deserve that.

FATHER
God is good, Imm el-Hassan. One child He chose for the honor of martyrdom. The other, God-willing, will be released and we'll see him before you know it. God is good.

MOTHER
God is good.

SAAD
May God rest his soul!

MOTHER
Hush! Don't say that! He's alive and he'll be released!

SAAD
I didn't mean it that way! I meant, like: Rest his soul! His living soul!

SAMAR
Sure, Saad. Come here, please?

SAAD *joins* SAMAR *downstage.*

SAAD
Why would you talk to me like that in front of your parents?

SAMAR
How do you want me to talk to you? You start saying random shit and kill my brother. It's bad enough he's locked up. And you keep getting in my dad's face. *Let's play cards, let's play cards.* Get your shit together.

SAAD
I'm sorry for trying to get your parents to like me.

SAMAR
Just…chill. You're acting like an ass. Anyway my parents don't like that kind of thing. Just be normal.

SAAD
You want normal? Why don't I just propose.

SAMAR
Saad. Don't be stupid. Are you insane? That's not how you propose.

SAAD
Fine. I'm leaving.

SAMAR
Don't be an idiot, Saad…

SAAD
(*Interrupting*) Do you all need anything?

MOTHER
Where are you going, dear? Dinner will be ready soon. You're going to leave without eating with us?

SAAD
I've gotta go. I'm supposed to meet someone. But I'll come by again in the next few days.

FATHER
Sure. Anytime. Walk him to the door, Wafi.

WAFI
He can walk himself to the door.

FATHER
Wafi. I said go. You want me to beat your ass?

SAAD *leaves.* SAMAR *joins her mother near the stove. Across the stage,* WAFI *and his* FATHER *are setting up the card game.*

WAFI
Look, he left. Did you really just threaten to beat my ass?

FATHER
You think I'm too old?

WAFI
Never mind. I'd rather beat you at cards.

FATHER
Ohhh, you think you can beat me at cards? Okay, mister. Shuffle and deal.

As they start playing cards, the conversation moves to SAMAR *and her* MOTHER.

MOTHER
So that was Saad.

SAMAR
(*Anxiously*) Please don't say you didn't like him.

MOTHER
He's ... young.

SAMAR
You should get to know him. Then we'll talk.

MOTHER
Okay but he is kind of young.

SAMAR
Better than being old.

MOTHER
I just worry about his ability to take care of you and your daughter. Think about this, Samar.

SAMAR
I'm in no rush. And I really do think he's up for it. From what I've seen. From what I know of him. He really loves me. And he's had a hard life, too. Just like my little girl. I'm not going to find a better fit.

MOTHER
Why would you say that? You're only 28, and you're gorgeous.

SAMAR
I'm divorced, Mom.

MOTHER
But this is Europe, sweetie.

SAMAR
Yes. This is Europe. And we're here with every single one of our family and friends who think divorced women are shameful and meant to disappear.

MOTHER
Says who? Has someone upset you?

SAMAR
So many people, mother. So many. You're new here. Soon you'll see what I mean. The shit we deal with.

MOTHER
Wow. Such optimism. Maybe give me ...fifteen minutes? To arrive and enjoy?

SAMAR
So he's young. But what else do you think of him?

MOTHER
He seems like ...a kind of ...basic ...kid. Oh God. Haha. See? "Kid."

SAMAR
Sure, he's just very ...simple. He doesn't really have friends, he doesn't really have problems either. He goes to work and he comes home. I love him. A lot, actually. And he loves me. And my daughter.

MOTHER
But honey, love will last maybe three years, and then it's over. This is your second time doing this. You need to think about it differently.

SAMAR
I need you to convince Dad.

MOTHER
I was going to say: you need to tell your father. You need to tell him this is the guy you want to marry. He thinks he's just a friend of yours and Wafi's. He finds out *I* know and haven't told him, I'll be the one getting divorced.

SAMAR
Amazing. Two divorcées. And then I won't need to tell you what a divorced woman's worth in Europe

They both laugh. The conversation moves to WAFI *and his* FATHER.

WAFI
Are you ready for me to beat you, Abu el-Hassan?

FATHER
I don't see it happening. Not in this lifetime.

WAFI
Who says I need a lifetime. I'll do it tonight.

FATHER
Damn. You remind me of your brothers. When you left the country you were a kid. Now you're a full-grown little punk.

WAFI
A proper man.

FATHER
You like it here?

WAFI
It's pretty awful. A little better since you got here, though.

FATHER
Really?

WAFI
I mean, it's okay. But we need a better living situation than this. The only place to smoke is under the stove vent, so we're literally living in the kitchen. And this city is a ghost town. We should go back to Aunt Obeida's city. You have people there. And after three years there, I know it well.

FATHER
Sure. But you have to give me a chance to arrive and figure things out a little bit. Once I have my feet under me everything will work itself out.

WAFI
And when do we think that'll be?

FATHER
I don't know. We'll see.

WAFI
Okay but listen, Abu el-Hassan. I'm about to lose credit for a whole other school year. They're telling me I can't take exams at this new

school because I didn't do my classes here. None of us want to be wasting our time.

FATHER
Don't tell me that, Wafi.

WAFI
I'm trying to sort it out. But if we go back to Aunt Obeida's city now, I can just go back to my old school. And everything will be okay.

FATHER
We'll talk about it later.

As WAFI *and his* FATHER *talk and play cards, the table is being set for dinner. Toward the end of the conversation,* SAMAR *and her* MOTHER *join the table.*

WAFI
Oh wow!

SAMAR
Listen to yourself. It's like I kept you starving.

WAFI
No, this is different. This is deep hunger. Ancient hunger. Refugee-camp hunger.

SAMAR
Don't remind me. What a nightmare.

MOTHER
What, you didn't eat at the camp?

WAFI
My first week in this country all I ate was crackers. I couldn't swallow the camp food. Then I couldn't get crackers. Eventually they moved me to another camp in Aunt Obeida's city. Thank God. After that I used to eat at her place.

MOTHER
Good Lord! Why didn't you tell us?

SAMAR
You had a lot to deal with.

MOTHER
We were really okay…

FATHER
Honestly. We could always eat.

SAMAR
Camp food was disgusting. They were hungry times. But I wish it was just the food.

MOTHER
Come on—what's more important than food?

WAFI
Well, then there was life with that asshole Samar was married to. His Lordship. The one we crossed the sea with.

FATHER
I still wish you hadn't gotten a divorce.

SAMAR
You don't know what he used to do to me.

MOTHER
I'm sure it was challenging for both of you.

WAFI
Man, he literally beat me up on the road. I was so upset I left and kept on alone. Crossed the forests by myself.

SAMAR
That day…God. Here's my little brother, who I'm responsible for, and here's my shitty husband, who starts blaming me for everything the minute we leave. He's just mad cause I insisted we bring our little

girl with us, and Wafi. For months all he wanted was to humiliate me. Like I was the enemy.

MOTHER

Good lord. Thank God you got rid of him.

FATHER

I understand the divorce. But I just wish it hadn't happened in such a rush …

SAMAR

In the camp he used to sleep all day. So I'm the one stuck watching our girl and bringing things to eat back to the room. God forbid we wake him up! Guys at the camp started saying he was just drunk all the time. Making all kinds of hints. Insinuations. And soon as it's clear I'm not interested, they turn it against me. Talking more shit, and worse. I'd just come back to the room and cry and cry, and His Highness is just barely waking up. *Go outside!* I tell him. *Show your face! They need to know I have a man! Please, for once, just make me feel like you care about my reputation!* But he would just smirk, like, *No smoke without fire, babe.* And if he didn't like how I talked to him he'd hit me.

FATHER *and* MOTHER *get up and clear their dishes, upset.* WAFI *continues to eat.*

WAFI

What? Don't get like that. We were having such a nice time.

MOTHER

It's alright, dear. Here, we'll finish eating. (*She serves everyone more food.*) It's just not easy for us to hear.

WAFI

Well, it wasn't easy for us to live. But now you're here and it's over. Let's eat, Samar. Poor Saad missed all this amazing food!

MOTHER

Saad seems nice. What do you think of him?

FATHER
The kid's an idiot. Why?

MOTHER
I'm just asking.

FATHER
I know you, you don't just ask things. What's going on?

SAMAR
Saad wants to propose to me.

FATHER
What?

SAMAR
If you don't approve, I'll drop it.

FATHER
(*Silence.*) It's not that I don't approve. I'm just surprised.

WAFI
So you approve?

FATHER
(*A tired laugh*) Approve? Approve of who? I barely know the guy.

MOTHER
It's okay. We'll talk about it later.

FATHER
Okay. Wait. No.

MOTHER
Please?

FATHER
Fine. No one lets me catch a breath in this house anyway.

Heavy silence.

SAMAR *and her* MOTHER *begin to clear the table.*

A knock at the door. AUNT OBEIDA *enters.*

OBEIDA
Blessed be, hello everyone.

FATHER
Blessed be, Obeida.

WAFI
Welcome, Abboud.

OBEIDA
How many times have I told you I don't like Abboud. Abboud is for boys.

SAMAR
That's quite a bag you've got with you, Auntie. Looks like you're here to stay?

OBEIDA
I have no desire to go back…His Royal Highness Prince of Princes is sulking again and wants to go back to Syria. I'm done with that conversation. I thought I'd come consult with you so I can figure out what to do.

WAFI
Oh he can go fuck himself.

FATHER
Hey. Language.

WAFI
She went through hell to get papers together for Family Reunification. It took her three years. Meanwhile he just waltzes over. He gets here. His wife knows the language. She's waiting for him, his home is ready, his socks are ready. And now for two months, he's whining and crying to everyone, he wants to go back to Syria, he can't live here, it's impossible. So he can go fuck himself. We haven't seen you smile, not once, since he got here.

FATHER
Good Lord.

MOTHER
Make yourself at home, Obeida. Get a divorce and come live with us. They say you walk into a room where people are eating, it means your mother-in-law must love you. We just finished eating. Your mother-in-law must hate you.

OBEIDA
I do think I'll divorce him. But I won't come here, you'll come stay with me. That house is in my name. God damn that mother-in-law. I'm starving. Oh, God forgive me.

SAMAR
Down with hunger, Auntie!

FATHER
Are you sure the windows are shut, Wafi?

WAFI
Locked. Absolutely sealed.

FATHER
I swear this wind is chilling my bones.

INTERLUDE ONE

FATHER

I've done my best, since I got here, to take advantage of the new situation. To start to make a better life so we can live in peace for once. In Syria I was a stonemason. Which is not easy work—the work can be harder than the stones themselves. And Lord knows there's no workers' comp. Something goes wrong, you might spend ten days at home after one day of work. God be praised.

But the employment office here said they wouldn't hire me as a stonemason. This is my trade, and I truly am a master of it, but they said I needed to start again. Do the training. They say, maybe try another line of work. I say okay. But then they tell me I'm too old, I'm not in good health. And then there's the question of this new language—I'm trying to learn, but I can barely speak. In the end they say why don't I work as a janitor. And eventually—once it's clear that every other door has been shut in my face—I say fine.

There's nothing wrong with cleaning. I know that. It's as honorable a job as any other. But I also know that back home you do that work, they treat you a little bit like a loser. My friends told me before I left, *Just you wait, you'll end up a garbage collector. Why else would they let people like us into their countries? Your own children will laugh at you.* And still—there's not a single one of these friends who wouldn't come here in a second if they could.

It eats my soul—the confusion of it all. Because they're right. Exactly what they said would happen, happened. And also, they're wrong. It's better here, it's not like working back home. Here you can really earn something. It's not the same. None of it. I don't know how to make sense of it.

ACT II

It's been a month since the parents arrived. Same space as Act I. Afternoon.

The FATHER *is reading the Quran alone in the kitchen. The* MOTHER *enters.*

FATHER
Amen. How was your nap?

MOTHER
Mmm.

FATHER
You seem off.

MOTHER
Bad dream.

FATHER
Nothing terrible, I hope?

MOTHER
Hassan was in heaven. Lush gardens everywhere. He was laughing. Suddenly Muwafak walked in and they started laughing together.

FATHER
It doesn't sound so bad. There are worse places than heaven.

MOTHER
Yes but I don't want Muwafak in heaven. I want Muwafak here, with me.

She weeps.

FATHER
Easy, Imm el-Hassan. Easy. It's a dream. You had a heavy lunch. Maybe you slept funny.

MOTHER
Then Wafi and Samar were there, too. And then Wafi was beating his brothers and heaven was a torture room in a detention camp.

FATHER
Oh God. Enough. Make yourself a cup of coffee and let yourself wake up.

MOTHER
I was desperate to wake up.

SAMAR *enters.*

FATHER
How was your nap, Sammour?

SAMAR
Long…I guess I slept a while. Saad says he wants to come have coffee.

FATHER
Now?

SAMAR
I can tell him not to, if that's not okay.

FATHER
It's okay. But tell him not to come.

SAMAR
What is that, a riddle?

FATHER
Do I look like I'm telling riddles?

SAMAR
No, seriously, I didn't understand.

FATHER
There's nothing to understand. He shouldn't come. Period.

MOTHER
Tell her why.

FATHER
Please stay out of it.

MOTHER
Fine. I'm out of it. But talk to your daughter.

SAMAR
Dad?

FATHER
We need to deal with this before he starts coming here all the time.

SAMAR
Exactly. So why don't you want him to come? What's the issue?

MOTHER
Where's your brother?

SAMAR
I just called him. He said he's on his way. He was at his friends' place.

FATHER
He has friends here?

MOTHER
Don't tell me he went all the way to Aunt Obeida's city…

SAMAR
He did.

FATHER
He thinks he lives alone? He can leave town without saying anything? What's wrong with you two?

MOTHER
Seriously! He acts like he lives alone.

SAMAR
Okay but that's a separate issue. That has nothing to do with me and Saad.

FATHER
That's where we disagree. To you it's separate, but actually it's the

same problem. With Wafi and with you. You run around like you don't owe anybody anything. And correct me if I'm wrong here but it doesn't seem like either of you has done a thing to improve your lives since you got here. I look at you both and I see failure after failure. Apparently Wafi's about to fail out of school—literally the only thing we've asked him not to do. And you're hopping from marriage, to divorce, to marriage, without thinking what any of it means for yourself or for your daughter. Have you thought about this? Even for a second? Why not learn the language? Find a job? Figure out how to support yourself? Then, sure, marry whoever the hell you want. And if he decides he wants a divorce, you can say kiss my ass and be fine.

SAMAR

Is that really what you want to say to me? Since you came here I've told you so many things—and that's all you've got? This whole time, it's been fucking miserable. All of it. Why can't you take our side for once? Be happy for what we've done. Stick up for us. But all you do is criticize and criticize. As though—excuse me—you have any right to be critical.

FATHER

I beg pardon! You're a little brat. A "right" to be "critical"? Who's the father here, me or you?

SAMAR

Sorry?

FATHER

Who's the father here, me or you?

SAMAR

You're the father.

FATHER

Exactly. I'm the father. So I decide.

SAMAR

You've barely seen the guy!

FATHER
I saw him and I didn't like him. He's a nothing. He's a loser. You think he can be responsible for you and your daughter? Him and his torn pants. The nerve. And here he comes, *Oh, let's play cards, let's play cards.* And now he wants to marry my daughter?

SAMAR
Okay your son wears the same pants.

FATHER
Which is why I have no plan to let him get married! Not before he learns to put on a decent pair of pants.

SAMAR
So it's the pants.

FATHER
The pants. Dear God: How is it you have seen fit to give my daughter a block of wood for a brain? *So it's the pants.* I tell her, *Go back to school.* I tell her, *Try to work, be independent.* And what does she say? She asks if it's the pants.

SAMAR
Look. I don't know what your problem with him is. But I don't think you can judge someone before you get to know him.

FATHER
I'm not talking about him. I could give two shits about this guy, bless his heart. I'm talking about you. I'm talking about your independence.

MOTHER
Okay, Samar. Drop it. You'll be the death of your father.

SAMAR
Fine. I'll keep my mouth shut.

Silence. FATHER*'s phone rings.*

FATHER
Hello? Yes. Hi. What? Okay, goodbye now. Goodbye, sir ... I'm sorry?

How else would you like me to speak to you? I'm tired of explaining that this is no way to solve the problem. Every time you get overwhelmed you pack your bag and announce that you're going back to Syria. It's a mess. How exactly is Obeida supposed to manage?

OBEIDA *enters from her nap.*

FATHER
She can suit herself? You're a shameless prick. Don't ever call this number again. Goodbye.

OBEIDA
Suit herself? Is that what he said? Or did I mishear?

FATHER
How was your nap, sister?

OBEIDA
Answer me, Abu el-Hassan.

FATHER
No, you didn't mishear.

MOTHER
He's just angry. Take it easy.

OBEIDA
Suit myself? After everything I've done? Son of a bitch. God forgive me. Suit myself? I worked and scraped and scrounged for three goddamn years. I lived like a dog. All so he could join me and have a life. A comfortable life. Suit myself? I don't understand! What have I done to hurt him? He says he can't live here. *It's unlivable.* Is that my fault? *It's unlivable here.* Guess what, *I* live here. I lived here three humiliating years, waiting for him. And while His Majesty was sitting pretty in Syria I traveled by desert and sea and almost died a million times to get here. He wants to go back? Fine. So let's figure out a way to stay together. Hell, let's figure out a way to separate. But this—*suit myself?* After all the hell I went through? What am I, an insect? At least you deal with an insect. You put it in a jar, you take it out. Or you kill it.

You don't say, *Suit yourself.*

MOTHER
(*Embracing* OBEIDA) Take it easy, Obeida. He's being a jackass. He probably didn't mean it. God will punish him.

OBEIDA
I will punish him. God willing.

FATHER
Easy, my dear. Let yourself calm down.

OBEIDA
I am calm. I'm going out for some fresh air. My ribs are on fire.

OBEIDA *exits.*

SAMAR
That's the difference between the ones who came after, through Family Reunification, and the ones who came first, like us. Whenever the ones who came after feel like it, they start complaining. *I want to go back to Syria*, they say. But for the ones like us, the ones who came first, there's no choice. This is our home, like it or not. People like us try to go back and we end up murdered in some police station. Syria doesn't want us anymore.

FATHER
Why would you say that to me?

SAMAR
Am I wrong?

FATHER
We came after. Through Family Reunification. Your mother and I did.

MOTHER
You're hard, Samar. You're awfully hard. And after everything you've seen. Be gentle with your father. He's dying here.

SAMAR

Hard…I don't think I'm hard. But God forgive you.

MOTHER

God forgive *us?*

SAMAR

Okay. This isn't going anywhere.

FATHER

I'll be the one to decide what's going anywhere. Don't you walk away when I talk to you. I don't approve of Saad. Not today, not tomorrow, not in a year. Go learn the language, go back to school, and when you can manage on your own, you can marry whoever you want. I'm not letting you get married while you're still so helpless. It'll just be your first marriage all over again.

SAMAR

Here we go. The same speech about how pathetic I am and what a terrible choice I made in my first marriage…

FATHER

You've been here three years. What have you done? You can't speak the language, you won't go back to school, you have no job. You have these trashy friends. What normal person could spend more than ten minutes with them?

SAMAR

I swear to God you're driving me insane. I've told you a thousand times how much shit I've been through in the last three years. How many more times do you want me to tell you? You're not wrong. But please. Just calm down. Just talk to me. I hear you, I'm with you, I promise things will go your way. Just…give me a chance.

FATHER

I don't understand what chance you're expecting us to give you at this point.

MOTHER

You say it like you haven't had a choice in the matter. You say it like we owe you something.

SAMAR

You don't...I owe it to myself...I don't know. I'm sorry. I'm confused. I don't know what you want me to say. I can't deal with this conversation anymore. I feel like I'm going crazy.

MOTHER

(*Sarcastically*) *You're* going crazy? If you're going crazy, what do you think we're feeling?

She laughs.

SAMAR

You're laughing? (*Yells*) The two of you are strangling me! Fuck this life and fuck God!

FATHER

You speak that way in front of me?

He slaps her.

SAMAR *runs to one of the knives, trying to kill herself.* FATHER *follows her. He shoves her and manages to grab the knife from her hand.* SAMAR *collapses, crying.*

FATHER

(*Beating himself up and yelling*) Pack my bags! Why the hell did I ever come here? I'm not staying a day longer. This bitch wants to drag me down with her.

WAFI *enters.*

WAFI

What's going on?

MOTHER
Oh, everything's fine.

FATHER
Where have you been, you little shit?

WAFI
Looking for a better home. For all of you. Better than this rat's nest. *What's going on?*

MOTHER
This one is threatening to kill herself if we don't let her marry Saad.

WAFI
Kill herself?

SAMAR *exits.*

FATHER
(*Yelling*) Samar!

WAFI
Just let her calm down. She'll be fine.

FATHER
And you, sir? Where the hell have you been?

WAFI
I went to Aunt Obeida's city. I found you an apartment. Through some friends. It's a one-bedroom with a kitchen. For now it'll work. There are Arabs there and you and Mom won't have to sit home all the time, bored. You haven't moved in a month. There you'll be able to enjoy. I'll be able to go back to school—and to my life. Everybody's moving there. Even Saad found a place.

FATHER
And who asked you to do all that?

WAFI
Don't talk to me like that.

MOTHER

(*With bitter sarcasm*) Well, Abu el-Hassan, you simply must show some respect to your son. (*Back to* WAFI) *Don't talk to me like that?* This is outrageous! We can't talk to either of you anymore! There are strangers in Syria who would treat us better than you do.

WAFI

I'm going to bed. It's impossible to have a conversation in this house.

FATHER

Goddamn the hour you offered to bring me to Europe.

WAFI *exits.*

FATHER

(*After a short silence*) Make me a cup of coffee.

MOTHER *stands and begins to prepare the coffee.*

MOTHER

I swear, Abu el-Hassan. I'm of two minds.

FATHER

What about?

MOTHER

On the one hand, I don't think we've done anything wrong. On the other hand, I say to myself, I've lost enough already. I still have two children. And I'll fight tooth and nail to keep my kids.

FATHER

Sure. It's why we left Syria and came here, isn't it? But look at them, neither shows us any respect. All we want is for them to be good. To be responsible. Independent.

MOTHER

But we should be good first. Shouldn't we?

FATHER

You don't think we're good to them?

MOTHER

That's not what I mean. We should be good. You and me. Not just good to them but good for ourselves. We're strangers here. The kids have grown. Maybe we should listen to them.

FATHER

If they spoke to us with a little respect, we'd listen to them.

MOTHER

Okay. So would you listen to me?

FATHER

All ears, ma'am.

MOTHER

Let Samar marry Saad. The guy seems fine enough. And at the end of the day, you reap what you sow.

FATHER

What the hell does that mean? Say he turns out like her ex-husband—who do you think will clean up the mess? Are we supposed to leave her to handle it all by herself?

MOTHER

Let's stay positive. She says the guy's decent, a hard worker, from a good family.

FATHER

After everything I've been through—at my age—forced out of my own country—I'm supposed to let our daughter twist my arm?

MOTHER

I don't think she's twisted it. Not yet. This is what I'm saying. All you did was offer a few objections and she nearly killed herself. Better to let her marry him with our blessing than against our will. There's nothing we can do anyway.

FATHER

We should have never fucking come here.

MOTHER
Here or there, it's the same. We can't keep putting everyone's lives on hold. The kids are growing. Wafi's a teenager. We see him on special occasions. We don't know anything about his life. I'm worried about him all the time. So let's move to the place he found for us. Let's have Samar live nearby. And let's see what happens.

INTERLUDE TWO

OBEIDA

I don't want to talk about how I got here. The humiliation along the way. Anyway you've heard that story a million times.

Now I teach kindergarten. Six months now. It's a very respectable job. The money is good. The people I work with are very sweet. When I need to leave early, they say, *Go, go, it's fine, we'll cover for you.* They don't let me wear myself out. And they're just so curious about people like us. They have so many questions. They want to know how we think, how we see the world.

I don't want to live alone. It makes me nervous. But I'm getting used to the idea. I haven't kept in touch with my family much. I don't have so much free time. Sometimes I reach out and we talk. Always in Arabic, though. They need to let that language go. It's time. We live here now. There's a certain kind of respect they need to learn for this country. This is where we live.

ACT III

Six months after the parents' arrival. The new home in the new city. The kitchen and its decor are the same, although the layout is different.

FATHER
I swear to God I'm this close to kicking everybody out. This is outrageous.

MOTHER
Calm down. It's fine. You can't kick anyone out. What would people think?

FATHER
It's too late to worry about that. He brought his friends. A bunch of teenagers. And they all fucking reek. A whole gaggle of wasted little punks at my daughter's jaha? And then here comes the father of the groom saying it's no big deal.

MOTHER
This is normal for people like them. Him and his trashy wife. And she starts yelling at us for being critical of his friends…

FATHER
Tell Wafi to serve the drinks and snacks and then let's get them out of here. It's over. As soon as we're done, we can deal with this jerk-off your daughter is inflicting on us.

MOTHER
Please. Just let him be. You know he's terrified of you. He's terrified because of how his friends are acting. He's just a pushover. He doesn't know what to do with himself.

FATHER
No, he's a total jackass. He's annoying. Laughing like a child. Bragging to his friends. Making idiotic jokes. I've had it. I'm going to deal with him. *And* his mother. Here trying to tell me *boys will be boys.*

MOTHER
Please tell me you didn't respond to that?

FATHER
Well, why don't you bring the-boys-who-will-be-boys over to your place. My home is not a place for drunks.

MOTHER
Good Lord. Please, just let it go. Just today. I promise things will go your way.

FATHER
Of course they will. This is the last time I let myself be forced into anything ever.

FATHER *exits.* MOTHER *calls* WAFI.

WAFI
Yes, Mom?

MOTHER
Here, bring these around.

WAFI
You're the best.

MOTHER
Wait. Come here. Now. What's that smell?

WAFI
What smell?

MOTHER
Your smell.

WAFI
What's wrong with my smell? Give me the tray. I don't want to leave our guests waiting.

MOTHER
I can't believe you. You've been drinking? Since when do you drink?

WAFI
What are you talking about? That's bullshit.

MOTHER

Don't talk to me like that, asshole! I'll deal with you later. Take the tray to the living room, serve the guests. Don't show your face to your father. If he smells you, he'll have a stroke.

WAFI

What smell?

MOTHER

Later. No time for this.

WAFI

I'm fed up. Everything I do is wrong.

MOTHER

Go on! And keep your mouth shut.

WAFI

Excuse me?!

MOTHER

Keep your mouth shut. Breathe through your ass if you have to. What comes out of there will smell better than what's coming out of your mouth.

WAFI

Enough already, Mom! And I thought I could talk to you about the way Dad treats me in front of people. It's not nice…

MOTHER

He thinks you've been drinking, too?

WAFI

What drinking? Where did you come up with this?

MOTHER

Take the tray and get out of here. I wouldn't blame him if he broke your skull.

WAFI *exits.* SAMAR *enters.*

MOTHER
Did you smell your brother?

SAMAR
Did you? Let's focus on the new catastrophe. Dad insisted on inviting Obeida's ex, and how he's going on and on about my dowry. He wants Dad to ask Saad for some insane amount.

MOTHER
I hope your father controlled his temper?

SAMAR
Sure. In front of the guests. But Dad proceeded to take this poor man outside and tell him to either shut up or fuck off. The ex did both.

MOTHER
Good Lord. How are we gonna make it up to your aunt?

SAMAR
Obeida? Oh I'm sure she's thrilled he's gone.

WAFI *enters.*

WAFI
You should come in there. You're missing out.

MOTHER
Shut the fuck up and don't let me see your face until this jaha is over. We'll talk later. Watch me kick your ass, you little punk. I'll take over the beating as soon as your father is done.

WAFI
Sure, sure. Oh, but it's a whole circus in there. One lame speech after another. The Sheikh doesn't know what he's doing. He's not officiating, he's just rambling, making shit up. It's pathetic. *As the Prophet says, as the Prophet says—Hold tight your purse.* The Prophet didn't say that. Someone must have slipped something into his drink.

MOTHER
So your father and I are the only sane ones left. We should get drunk,

pop some pills, and then maybe we'd be able to keep up.

WAFI
And Aunt Obeida's flirting with literally everyone. What's up with that? Her husband's gone. Her makeup is all smudged.

SAMAR
Stop saying *her husband*! Her ex. She couldn't stand him anymore so she divorced him. He couldn't keep his mouth shut so your father kicked him out.

WAFI
I thought he left because of Obeida.

SAMAR
People are starting to leave.

MOTHER
Good Lord.

Enter the FATHER, SAAD, *and* OBEIDA.

FATHER
And the cherry on top was that asshole of a Sheikh!

OBEIDA
Don't talk about the Sheikh that way.

FATHER
He can go fuck himself.

SAAD
Easy, uncle.

FATHER
As for you I was about ready to smash your face. And I would have if it didn't mean people would say I ruined my own daughter's jaha. Who the hell are these demons you invited?

SAAD
I mentioned it to two guys. Decent guys. They brought their friends.

They said they wanted to celebrate with me. But the friends are not… good. What am I supposed to do? I don't know half of these people.

SAMAR
It's your fault.

SAAD
(*Yells at her*) How is it my fault? What would you have wanted me to do, Miss Samar?

FATHER
And why are you yelling at her?

SAAD
I'm not yelling at her. But she knows perfectly well I had nothing to do with it. And now she's making it my fault—in front of you!

OBEIDA
You can't always choose who shows up, when people are thrown together like this.

MOTHER
Never mind. Congratulations, you two.

All embrace SAAD *and* SAMAR *and congratulate them.*

SAMAR
(*To* SAAD) Why didn't your parents stay?

SAAD
They wanted to bring my uncle home.

OBEIDA
Why, does he live alone?

SAAD
He does.

SAMAR
His wife ran off with her lover.

FATHER
Is this the drunk uncle?

OBEIDA
Listen, he's not a drunk.

MOTHER
And what makes you so sure of that, my dear?

OBEIDA
(*Embarrassed*) I ...don't know. It just didn't seem that way.

FATHER
Anyway ...

OBEIDA
What does your uncle do?

The FATHER *gives her a confused look. She keeps quiet.*

WAFI
I wanna go see my friends. They're waiting for me.

FATHER
You realize that since we came to this magnificent city—the city to which Your Lordship has brought us—we never see you?

MOTHER
If only that was the issue.

FATHER
What?

MOTHER
Nothing. I just heard a lot of promises before we came. (*Sarcastically*) I'll start studying ...I'll work ...I'll stay home. Let's just move there ...

OBEIDA
Oh please. Let him enjoy his youth.

FATHER
You seem to be the one enjoying your youth today.

OBEIDA
It's a celebration! How do you want me to be?

SAMAR
So you're all chipper because of me and Saad?

OBEIDA
Samar! What a question! Forgive me, Lord.

SAMAR
I'm kidding! What's wrong with you?

SAAD
Please, uncle. Don't be mad at me. Are we good?

FATHER
We're good. You little punk.

Everyone laughs except the MOTHER *and the* FATHER.

FATHER
Don't you want to get married, Wafi?

WAFI
Why would I do that?

FATHER
So your mother and I can go back to Syria.

MOTHER
You can go back, darling. I'll stay here. I'll be done with Language Level 1 in a few months.

FATHER
I see. So it's not just my kids I've lost to Europe.

WAFI
Man, what do you mean *lost*? What are we, house keys?

MOTHER
You, shut the fuck up.

FATHER
What's going on? I feel like you've done something and no one is telling me.

MOTHER
It's nothing. Really. Enough with the Syria business. Please.

FATHER
Nothing I've seen of this country makes me want to stop talking about Syria. So stay. Obeida will go back home with me.

OBEIDA
(*Laughs conspicuously*) Me? You couldn't pay me to leave. The day I leave this city it'll be in a coffin. Go back to Syria? Give me a break.

SAAD
Seems like you like it here.

SAMAR
Poor woman. I don't know what she's seen to make her like it so much.

OBEIDA
It's not about what I've seen. It's what I will see. The future will be better, God willing.

MOTHER
Bless His name.

OBEIDA
God forgive us.

MOTHER
Did I say something wrong?

OBEIDA
I can ask for forgiveness, it doesn't mean you blasphemed. There's a Sheikh on YouTube who says—

FATHER
A lesson in religion. Just what we need.

SAAD
I gotta go, uncle. Do you need anything from me?

OBEIDA
Are you going to your uncle's?

SAAD
I am. Should I drop you off on my way?

OBEIDA
Oh, where does he live?

SAAD
Other side of town. Last bus stop.

OBEIDA
(*Laughs*) How will you drop me off?

SAAD
You have a point.

SAMAR
It's fine. He'll drop you off and go back.

OBEIDA
It's okay, dear. I'll stay for a bit. Wafi will drop me off.

SAMAR
Good, yes, spend the night with us. We need to gossip.

MOTHER
Stay. You have something else to do?

OBEIDA
Fine. Thank you, Saad.

SAAD
Of course.

WAFI
Wait, I'll come down with you. Bye.

WAFI and SAAD exit. The FATHER and the MOTHER watch YouTube. Neither uses headphones. From the MOTHER's phone we hear a Syrian soap opera. From the FATHER's, the running commentary on a soccer game. Each tries to raise the volume.

SAMAR
Put on your headphones.

MOTHER
Sure.

The MOTHER puts on her earphones and gives the FATHER his.

SAMAR
What's the story with Saad's uncle?

OBEIDA
Which uncle?

SAMAR
What do you mean, which uncle? There's more than one you're in love with?

OBEIDA
Oh, shut up. God forgive me.

SAMAR
So, Sheikha Obeida. You're in love.

OBEIDA
Not love. But he is cute, isn't he?

SAMAR
Don't.

OBEIDA
Really? Why not?

SAMAR
He hit his wife so much she ran away. Now he's telling everyone she ran off with some lover.

OBEIDA
She must have done something for him to want to hit her. It's not fair to judge people.

SAMAR
Are you out of your mind?

OBEIDA
And how are you so sure he used to hit her?

SAMAR
Everybody knows.

OBEIDA
Who's to know what happens between a man and his wife?

SAMAR
Most of the time you don't. But when it gets bad enough, people know. At least wait till you're done with the first one.

OBEIDA
You didn't wait very long, did you? God forgive you.

SAMAR
Hey! What do you mean? Forgive me for what?

OBEIDA
Oh, nothing. Don't be upset.

SAMAR
It's fine. But believe me. You don't want to end up with this guy.

OBEIDA
Oh, he hasn't even proposed yet.

SAMAR
Proposed? So you've really been talking?

OBEIDA
Just once. I met him at language school. He offered to help me learn. I wasn't particularly friendly at the time.

SAMAR
Okay.

OBEIDA
And today he slips me his number on the way out. He had his eyes on me the whole party. What do you think? He loves me, right? God forgive me.

SAMAR
Listen, Auntie. The guy is no good. I'm telling you. I know him.

OBEIDA
Well, he's a man. Like any man. Say it's true what people say. A little tenderness will set him straight.

SAMAR
What *people* say? What *I* say!

OBEIDA
Listen, honey: I'm a divorced woman. I can't live alone and have my reputation go down the drain. God forbid. And anyway I like him. Really. The first time I saw him he did something to me. He looked at me and I left the earth a little bit. Oh, God forgive me. I don't know what I'm talking about.

SAMAR
Well, sounds like fun times ahead.

OBEIDA
It'll be okay.

Now SAMAR *and* OBEIDA *each play different songs on their phones.* OBEIDA *plays "Albi w Muftahu" by Farid el-Atrash.* SAMAR *plays "Ishq Mawt" by Saif Nabeel. Each wears headphones. For a while, silence on stage. Each character on their own phone, distracted. Eventually, a chaotic blend of all the sounds is heard through the sound system.*

Then WAFI *enters wearing his own earphones and we hear "Guerilla" by Soolking.*

INTERLUDE THREE

WAFI

I tried to be the son they wanted. But I failed. By the time I was thirteen I was living alone. And I lived alone until I was sixteen. I learned everything a kid isn't supposed to learn—smoking, drinking, drugs—in the best place to learn all that shit: a refugee camp for minors. If you want to learn how to become a thug, try a refugee camp.

I wasted my school years there, waiting for my parents to show up. I grew up without them. I had friends from every one of the most miserable places on earth. And I watched every one of them start dealing. Get wrapped up in worse and worse shit. Some of them became the gang's assassins. It's helpful for the gang leaders, cuz the law is easier on minors.

Anyway most of the camp isn't really minors. They're adults. You can tell, just looking at them, but they tweak the ages on their documents so they can send for their families later on. You can imagine the kind of shit that goes on. The men are all horny. They can't find women. You're supposed to be strong. Tough. You're supposed to out-tough the gang leader. And that's why you can't stay clean, the way your parents want you to. But still, you're a kid. How bad can you can fuck up? With everything I did wrong, I was still just waiting for my parents to come, thinking they would save me. Maybe that was the biggest fuck-up of all.

So I left. And now here I am, drifting. Sometimes I hit. Sometimes I miss. Sometimes it works out. Sometimes it doesn't. God knows I love you. So much. And care for you. It's not how I wanted to leave home. With you begging me to stay.

INTERLUDE FOUR

SAMAR

Saad and I had a boy and now I'm pregnant with a girl. A while ago, Social Services started investigating us because my eldest daughter said at school that I hit her. I only hit her once, but that was enough. Me, my husband, and my ex all got dragged into these endless interrogations. They interrogated Saad and my little boy. They basically interrogated my unborn girl. Thank God they closed the case. The kids will stay with me.

Social Services had been saying they were going to take the kids away. They said they were looking for a safe environment, that they were going to place them with foster families—or honestly, probably in camps.

I know I'm not the perfect mother. I'm not a perfect wife, either, or a perfect person. But all I want is to start a family.

It's impossible here. Or maybe it's just different. Either way I don't know how. Maybe this was why my father wanted me to go back to school, find a job, figure out my life, before I did anything else. But even that is not so easy. The people who manage to do it, they're poster children, they're big news. We fled Hell. And now we only have two options: become a poster child, or a fuck-up. And with fuck-ups like me, they can take it all away. Our lives, our minds, our souls, our children.

ACT IV

Two years after the arrival of the parents. Same set as Act III. The FATHER *and the* MOTHER *sit in the kitchen.* MOTHER *types on her mobile.*

FATHER
Who are you texting, this late?

MOTHER
No one. I'm translating. I want to learn a few more words. You don't talk to any of your friends in Syria anymore.

FATHER
They can all go fuck themselves. It's too much. Whenever I talk with one of those motherfuckers it just makes me feel even further away.

MOTHER
Really?

FATHER
It's the same two complaints a thousand different ways. You and I ran off, happy-go-lucky, to the place where money grows on trees. They're the noble ones, toughing it out. But still—they wish they had it like we did. I don't know how to respond. They don't get it. They don't see the contradiction. Every time I talk to them. It's a dead end.

MOTHER
You realize you're just cutting yourself off from the world...

FATHER
I don't even know what world I live in anymore. I want to tell them that I'm dying but I don't know how to say it. I can picture their glee. They'll think I'm being a brat. They'll think compared to theirs my problems are ridiculous.

MOTHER
Stop. Look at yourself. You're stuck. This isn't going anywhere. Even when people visit, you just get mad and end the conversation.

FATHER
I'm not interested anymore. In anything.

MOTHER
Sure. But these are friends you've known your whole life.

FATHER
To hell with this life and to hell with how we've lived it. And anyway what am I supposed to tell them? That I came here and stopped being able to recognize my own kids? They warned me that would happen. *Of course not,* I told them. *I know my kids. I know how I raised them.*

MOTHER
Europe didn't change your kids. Your kids grew up.

FATHER
Do you really believe that? Or do you just want to believe it? The way I spend all my time trying to believe in any number of things?

MOTHER
We have to get used to things. And there are some things that we need to look at differently. Not the way we're used to looking at them.

FATHER
Now? At this age? So I'll call my friends and tell them I barely see my son. That when I do his breath stinks of alcohol. That I act like I don't smell it because I know perfectly well I can't control him. That I'm falling apart. *You should be grateful,* they'll say. *You have a monthly income. You have what you need to live. You have electricity, water, heat…*

MOTHER
They're right.

FATHER
Of course they're right. And I'm right. And you're right. And Wafi and Samar are right. But why are we all in so much pain?

MOTHER
I wish I knew.

WAFI *walks in and sits silently.*

MOTHER
What's wrong, Wafi?

WAFI
I almost drowned. My friends took me to go swimming. So I could get over my fear of the ocean. The moment I got in I went stiff. The first time I saw the ocean I almost drowned. It all came flooding back.

FATHER
That's all past.

WAFI
Like the present is any better.

MOTHER
Wow. Coming from you ...

FATHER
You're the one living the good life.

WAFI
That's what you think?

FATHER
Am I wrong?

WAFI
It's not just the one year of school I lost. It's years. My classmates are children. None of them speak my language. I'm sick of this school. I just want work, any kind of work. But no one will hire me. Not legal work, and nothing under the table either. I know two kinds of people here. There are the kids who are from here and they're my age but you can't even begin to imagine their lives. You'd never approve. And then there are the kids like me, miserable, spending all our time depressed, trying desperately to be happy. And deep down we know we'll always just be trying. And then there's you. I don't know how to make you proud of me. No matter what I do, some part of me feels not good enough. There's this anger inside me. I don't know how to let it out. I'm afraid to let it out.

MOTHER
Is all that really true, Wafi?

SAMAR and OBEIDA walk in. A bruise on SAMAR's face.

OBEIDA
Hello.

FATHER
Hey.

MOTHER
What happened to your face, Samar?

SAMAR
Kitchen cupboard.

FATHER
Are you sure?

SAMAR
What else would it be?

WAFI
Tell me who hit you and I'll stab his eyes out.

SAMAR
No one hit me.

FATHER
Not your husband?

SAMAR
Not my husband.

FATHER
I'm not an idiot. I may let things slide, but I'm not an idiot.

MOTHER
Please calm down.

FATHER

I've been calm for too long. I can't take it anymore! What cupboard leaves fist-shaped bruises? Your husband is a creep and we all know he's a creep. He's a creep and a child. Answer me! Is he the one who hit you?

SAMAR

I'm leaving.

FATHER

Don't you dare. Come over here. I'm not some son of a bitch you turn your back on when I'm trying to talk to you. I warned you about him. Over and over. Over and over and over. You're scared to stay with him because he'll hit you and you're scared to leave because what would it look like to get a divorce so soon, and for the second time, too. And this is where your stubbornness has landed you. I told you not to marry that asshole. You thought I had a problem with his pants. I wish you would all get your heads on straight and listen to me for once!

SAMAR

Listen. I've been meaning to say this since the day you arrived. I don't owe anyone anything. Not even God. When have you ever had my back? When have you made me feel like I could rely on you? You sit all day doing nothing. You sit, and warn, and criticize, and complain. What fabulous things have you achieved in your life that you expect us to do so much? Dude, if you had raised us in better conditions we wouldn't have ended up here. You threw us in the sea so we could bring you over afterwards. And then you get here and you start ordering us around. No room to mess up, to try things, to date. Our life is already a mess. You're just making it worse. Saad hit my daughter. I waited for her father to come to pick her up. When Saad and I were alone, I tried to talk to him. Then he tried to come after me. So I came after him.

FATHER

You came after him?

SAMAR
But this time I had a knife.

Long silence.

FATHER
Shut the windows.

MOTHER
They've been shut a very long time.

CONTRIBUTORS

Yasser Abu Shaqra is a Palestinian-Syrian playwright, born in Damascus and a graduate of the Higher Institute of Dramatic Arts. He designed and implemented several interactive theater projects in Damascus and its suburbs. His plays have been published and performed internationally, and a collection of his poetry was released in Denmark. He currently resides in France. He works as the scientific editor of the Theater Section in the Arabic encyclopedia *Arabica.*

Lucas Baisch is from San Francisco. His plays have been read and developed at the Goodman Theatre, The Playwrights' Center, The Bushwick Starr, The Mercury Store, First Floor Theater, Cutting Ball Theater, Playwrights Horizons, Clubbed Thumb, The Neo-Futurists, Chicago Dramatists, etc. Lucas is a recipient of a Steinberg Playwright Award, the Princess Grace Award in Playwriting, a Jerome Fellowship, the Kennedy Center's KCACTF Latinx Playwriting Award, and the Chesley/Bumbalo Playwriting Award. His plays have been published by Bloomsbury/Methuen Drama, Yale's *Theater* Magazine, and 53rd State Press. Outside of writing for theatre, his artwork has been presented at Elsewhere Museum, the Electronic Literature Organization, gallery no one, and the RISD Museum. He has held residencies through Ars Nova, Page 73, the Lower Manhattan Cultural Council, ACRE, Elsewhere Museum, Millay Arts, the Wurlitzer Foundation, the Djerassi Resident Artists Program, the Goodman Theatre's Playwrights Unit, and as a Lambda Literary Playwriting Fellow. MFA: Brown University.

Jess Barbagallo is a theater artist and poet based in New York City. He has been staging his writing for many years with his friends, students, and loves: *Grey-Eyed Dogs, Karen Davis Does the Club, Etc., Good Year for Hunters My Old Man and Other Stories, Beaches in Winter, Weekend at Barry's/ Lesbian Lighthouse, Laughing in Los Angeles,* and *Cemetery Soup.* Other directing credits include *Pony* (Portland Theater Festival), *It's That Time of the Month* (Soho Rep, Obie Award - Special Citation), and *The Last Podcast on Earth* (The Tank). Jess has recently performed in Agnes Borinsky's *The Trees,* Amanda Horowitz's *Bad Stars,* Jerry Lieblich's *The Barbarians,* and Jordan Baum's *21st Century Princess.* He considers himself a proud member of a community of stage-makers who push against theatrical norms to reflect life in 2025.

Jordan Baum writes and makes theater. Most recently, he wrote and directed *21st Century Princess*, which was performed at Pageant In NYC in 2025.

Executive Director of EnviroFest and President/Founder of Tunisia Cinema Foundation, **Hisham Ben Khamsa** is a cultural activist, specialist in communication and cinema and a veteran of the Tunisian, Arab and African film industry. For many years and until 2019, he was the communication director of the Carthage Film Festival JCC. In 2007, he founded the Tunisian Cinema Pavilion at the Cannes Film Festival on behalf of the Tunisian Ministry of Culture. Hisham is also a translator and subtitler from and into English, French and Arabic of Tunisian and international films selected and awarded at the biggest festivals in the world, Cannes, Venice, Toronto, the French Césars and the Oscars. He has previously collaborated with Leila Toubel, translating two of her plays.

Agnes Borinsky is a writer, performer, and convener of people. Her plays include *The Trees, A Song of Songs, Of Government, Ding Dong It's the Ocean, Brief Chronicle, Books 6-8*, and *Lost Tribe.* Participatory projects include: *Working Group for a New Spirit* and *Weird Classrooms.* With Paul Spera, she is co-custodian of Masrah Ensemble.

Jonas Elbousty holds an MPhil and a PhD from Columbia University. He is an academic, writer, and literary critic and translator. He teaches in the Department of Near Eastern Languages and Civilizations at Yale University. He is the author or co-author of nine books, including *Faces* (Georgetown University Press, 2024), *Reading Mohamed Choukri's Narratives* (Routledge, 2024), *The Screams of War* (Seagull Books, 2024), *Tales of Tangier* (Yale University Press, 2023), *Aswat Mu'asira: Short Stories* (Georgetown University Press, 2023), *Vitality and Dynamism: Interstitial Dialogues of Language, Politics, and Religion in Morocco's Literary Tradition* (Leiden University Press, 2014). He is the book series editor of *the Cultural Production on the Middle East and North Africa*, and editor in chief of *the Journal on Maghrebi Studies.* His forthcoming books are *Zoco Chico* (Georgetown University), *The Routledge Handbook on Cultural Production in the Middle East and North Africa* (Routledge), and *Exploring Contemporary Arabic Novels* (Routledge).

Since she earned her PhD in theatre from the Sorbonne-Paris (1982), **Hanan Kassab Hassan** has been a tenured professor at the Damascus University in Syria, in addition to several professorships in the Higher Institute of Dramatic Arts (HIDA) in Damascus, and in the Saint Joseph University in Beirut (IESAV). She was the General Manager of the Damascus Opera House, the General Secretary of *Damascus Arab Capital of Culture 2008*, and the Dean of the Higher Institute of Dramatic Arts. She was also a member of the "Conseil Cuturel de l'Union Pour la Méditerranée" in France, and an external evaluator for cultural projects presented to the IFPC, UNESCO, the Kuwait Prize, and the Doha Drama Writing Award. She was chosen as an individual consultant for the Intangible Cultural Heritage Section of UNESCO (2016). She has directed theatre plays, managed workshops on dramaturgy, and written many research papers in the fields of theater and the arts. She translated from French into Arabic and vice versa several essays, novels and theatrical texts. She is co-author of the *Dictionary of Terms and Concepts of Drama and Performing Arts,* which is one of the main references in the field of theatre in the Arab world.

Nazareth Hassan is an interdisciplinary artist working in performance, writing, music, video, and photography. Recent performance works include *Untitled (1-5)* at The Shed (text published by 3 Hole Press), *VANTABLACK* at Theatretreffen Stuckemarkt in Berlin, *Slow Mania 009* at Center for Performance Research in Brooklyn, and *Memory A* at Museo Universitario del Arte Contemporaneo in Mexico City. Their first collection of poetry and photography *Slow Mania* will be published in 2025 by Futurepoem. They have released 4 singles, available on all platforms. They were the 2022 resident dramaturg at the Royal Court Theatre in London. They are a 2023-25 Jerome Hill artist fellow, and a current resident of the Vineyard Theatre.

Wael Kadour is a Syrian playwright and director based in France. He wrote and directed the play *Chapitre quatre*, in the official program of the 2025 Avignon Festival. In the same year, he presented *Braveheart* at the Theater an der ruhr in Germany and Choisy-le-Roi in France. He has been the artistic director of the Ma'louba Theater Collective since 2022, where he has produced and participated in several plays, including *The Long Shadow of Alois Brunner*, directed by Omar Elerian, which opened at the Euroscene Festival in Leipzig in 2023, and *Up There* at the Theater an der ruhr and Theaterhaus Jena in Germany. His plays have been presented in Italy at the Naples Festival, the Kunstfest Weimar in Germany, and Les Vagamondes Mulhouse Festival in France, in addition to Egypt and Lebanon. He has participated as an artistic collaborator and facilitator in several theater labs, workshops, artist residencies, and theater readings in Europe, the United States, the Arab region, Africa, and the United Kingdom.

Arzé Khodr was born in Beirut, Lebanon, in 1976 and graduated in Theatre Studies from Saint Joseph University (Beirut) in 1999. She is a playwright and has worked as a writer and content creator for television since 2005. Her first play, *The House* (2008), was translated from Arabic and published in English and French. It was performed in German at the Zimmertheater in Tübingen, Germany, in 2014. In 2018, *The House* was staged in Beirut, where Khodr won the award for Best Playwright at the Lebanese National Theatre Festival. In 2023, her play *The Smell of Jasmine* was selected as the Middle East regional winner of the BBC International Radio Playwriting Competition.

Haruna Lee is a Taiwanese/Japanese/American theater maker, screenwriter, educator and community steward. Plays include *War Lesbian*, *Memory Retrograde*, *plural (love)* and *Suicide Forest* for which they received an Obie Award for Playwriting and Conception and was on the 2020 Kilroys List. Lee has received the Steinberg Playwright Award, the Ollie New Play Award, FCA Grants to Artists Award, a MacDowell Fellowship, the Map Fund Grant, and is a member of New Dramatists. Their writing has been published by 53rd State Press, Theater Magazine, Table Work Press and Almanac, and they've taught playwriting and theater at Brooklyn College, Stanford, NYU, Pace, and York College.

Rim Mejdi (b. 1989, Marrakech) is a Moroccan filmmaker, theatre director, and curator. Her work unfolds across cinema, performance, and visual arts, weaving together narratives that explore intimacy, adolescence, and the body in moments of transition. Through these themes, she investigates how personal experiences resonate with collective histories. Her artistic research extends to the urban and peri-urban landscapes of Marrakech and its surroundings, which she approaches as body-territories marked by rupture and transformation. These spaces become central to her reflections on memory, nature, and the imprint of capitalist hegemony, manifested through tourism, gentrification, and extractivism. Working fluidly between film, photography, and performance, Mejdi develops a practice attentive to both individual and communal experience. Her projects seek to map fragile thresholds—between childhood and adulthood, private and public, body and territory—while engaging with contemporary artistic and cinematic practices in Morocco and beyond.

A Tunisian novelist, poet, visual artist, and researcher, **Sami Nasr** won the 2015 Sharjah Novel Award for *Tales of Jaber the Shepherd* (Waraq Publishing House, UAE, 2014) and the 2017 Katara Novel Award for *The Human Bird* (Katara Books, Qatar, 2018). He was shortlisted for the Ghassan Kanafani Novel Award for *Barlatras* (2024) and the Golden Narrative Award for his short story collection *The Assassins* (2024). He is founder and editor-in-chief of the peer-reviewed quarterly *Al-Shair Magazine*. An internationally accredited narrative trainer and supervisor of the "Workshop" short story project, he has published nine books of poetry, five novels, one play, three books of criticism, and two poems in two multilingual anthologies. His research and creative writing focus on oral narratives, exploring their potential and energy within his fictional worlds.

Caline Nasrallah is a literary translator, editor, and researcher based between Montreal and Beirut. Her extensive editing and translation work spans fiction and non-fiction. She has been published with Syracuse University Press, *Wasafiri*, Interlink Publishing, and more.

Clem Naylor studied Arabic at Oxford University and at Damascus

University. He started translating plays for the Royal Court Theatre in London in 2008 and has continued to translate Arabic plays on and off since then, including the works of Mohammad Al Attar, Dalia Taha, and Arzé Khodr. Alongside his translation work, Clem's work as a British diplomat has taken him to Cairo, Bamako and Berlin.

Leila Toubel is a self-taught Tunisian actress, playwright, director, and activist, recognized as one of the leading figures of Tunisian theatre. Born in 1962 in Hammam-Lif, she worked for twenty-five years alongside Ezzeddine Gannoun, notably as Artistic Director of El Hamra Theater. In 2014, she founded *Resist'Art* and later launched *Dreams Chebeb*, a support program for young creators in Tunisia. Her acclaimed trilogy—*Solwen*, *Hourya*, and *Yakouta*—as well as her latest play *Ad Vitam* (2025) blend poetic imagery with social engagement, exploring memory, life and death, human fragility, and freedom. Known for her uncompromising stance against obscurantism and violence, particularly towards women, she embraces a profound connection with the Tunisian dialect, expressed through a raw, deeply emotional writing style. She has performed on stages around the world, from Tokyo to Montreal. For Toubel, theatre remains "the greatest and shortest love story between an actress and a spectator—divine, ephemeral, and eternal."

ABOUT MASRAH ENSEMBLE

Masrah Ensemble is a nonprofit theatre company and organization that makes, develops, and fosters research and criticism of theatre with a focus on the Arab stage. The Ensemble aims to reconfigure audiences and to encourage transcendent, riveting theatre.

2009 – Founded by Eyad Houssami in Beirut, Lebanon.

2009–12 – Theater of Desire cabaret

The Cabaret began in 2009, occurring six times in residences, and was revived with the arts organization 98Weeks, which hosted the Cabaret in their space. We co-presented five Cabarets in 2011 and one Cabaret in 2012. Each event drew around 35 attendees and featured several performances by amateurs and professionals, young and old—in Arabic, French, and English. Cabarets were followed by discussions between audiences and artists.

2011 – Play readings

Masrah Ensemble staged two readings of new plays by emerging writers. In 2011, Raphael Khouri directed a reading from *Tennis in Nablus* by Palestinian-American playwright Ismail Khalidi, and moderated the talkback with Khalidi, which drew around 45 individuals. In 2012, Eyad Houssami directed a reading from *Damascus-Aleppo*, a new Arabic play by Syrian playwright Abdullah Al Kafri, followed by a talkback for an audience of a few dozen.

2012 – *Doomed by Hope*

Masrah Ensemble edited and launched the first English-Arabic volume on Arab theatre, *Doomed by Hope: Essays on Arab Theatre* (Pluto Press and Dar al-Adab). The release of the publication coincided with an international theatre series with events and programs in Lebanon, Australia, The Netherlands, and the United States.

2013 – *Mud*

A play in 17 scenes
By María Irene Fornés
With Mohammad Akil, Clare Barron, and Julian Farhat
Directed by Eyad Houssami
Co-Produced by Nagham Abboud and Jowe Harfouche
Performed in Arabic and English

Masrah Ensemble presented more than a dozen performances of *Mud* in

Mansion, a former Ottoman residence-cum-creative space in Beirut, Lebanon, in February and March 2013. The actors performed in a room on the second floor of the dilapidated residence that sat about twenty people. The performances were free of charge and followed by a candlelit Ethiopian dinner. In pursuit of our mission to "reconfigure audiences," we were pleased to welcome and meet diverse audiences that mingled traditional theatergoers with domestic workers, refugees, and laborers throughout the entire project.

2014–15 – Triangles

Triangles was a festival-in-progress that translated, workshopped, and re-imagined three plays through a series of residencies and public encounters in Beirut and New York and an array of collaborations with groups and artists in Lebanon, Syria, Iraq, the United States, and beyond. With collaborations between artists and co-conspirators Yasser Abu Shaqra, Eyad Houssami, Agnes Borinsky, and Rahel Zegaye, we considered how language and the act of translation could occasion creative play between artists, students, and organizers, and communities of English-, Arabic-, and Amharic-speakers in Lebanon and the US. Hadi Deaibess and Ferdaous Naili were essential collaborators on the festival as well.

Texts included:

Yasser Abu Shaqra, *Before Dinner*
  Translated from Arabic to English by Samar Awada
  presented in Arabic and English at Lebanese American University (Beirut) and Ensemble Studio Theater (New York)

Agnes Borinsky, *Baltimore*
  Translated from English to Arabic by Fadi Tofeili
  presented in English and Arabic by Agnes Borinsky and Daniel Balabane at Mansion (Beirut) and Alwan for the Arts (New York)

Tsegaye Gabre-Medhin (1936–2006), *Yekermo Sew (Tomorrow's Man)*
  Translated from Amharic to English by Nafkote Tamirat
  Translated collaboratively from English to Arabic by students at the American University of Beirut
  Presented in English, Amharic, and Arabic at the Migrant Workers Community Center (Beirut) and the Nuyorican Poets Cafe (New York)

2015–16 – Family Ti-Jean

A street theatre project, educational program, and cultural initiative confronting the divisive repercussions of post-colonial warfare, *Family Ti-Jean* was a musical theatre project in public spaces. It was developed and presented by amateur teenage and professional adult actors and musicians representing various communities: Syrian and Palestinian refugees, Lebanese citizens, migrant workers, and international artists. Masrah Ensemble partnered with Basmeh & Zeitooneh for Relief and Development in Shatila refugee camp, and the latter's Art and Culture Center served as the base for the project. The collaboration between the two institutions ran the course of about one year. Featuring adaptations of a Caribbean and a Serbian play, the double-bill theatre project concerned the welfare of youth and women as well as of refugees and migrant workers who suffer human rights violations and discrimination in Lebanon. It culminated in spring 2016 with free performances, directed by Eyad Houssami, at six locations throughout Beirut, including public parks and open community centers, and reached well over a thousand people. Family Ti-Jean intermingled demographic groups otherwise at odds in a society on the periphery of the ongoing Syria war; indeed, Beirut is mired in segregation, inequality, and internecine tension, echoes of the Lebanese Civil War (1975–1990).

2017 – MARSAH.ORG

Masrah Ensemble launched marsah.org, an online publishing platform that archived the many theatrical translations that had been byproducts of the company's work over the years.

2018 – Berlin Summit

In 2018, Milia Ayache, Agnes Borinsky, Yasmin Hafesji, Eyad Houssami, Ahmed Masoud, Esther Neitzel, and Paul Spera gathered in Berlin to consider the future of the company. Agnes and Paul become volunteer co-custodians.

2021–25 – Open Call

In May 2021, Masrah Ensemble released an Open Call for new plays in Arabic. Formulated by Yasser Abu Shaqra, the response was a flood of texts—almost 500 submissions from all over the Arabic-speaking world. A jury of five—Yasser, Faisal Hamadah, Nejma Zeghidi, Eid Aziz, and Sara Fakhry Ismail—selected five texts. Those five texts became the core of the present anthology, where they are joined by co-editor Abu Shaqra's *Left Out Gone Bad*. 53rd State Press collaborated with Masrah Ensemble to publish the plays in both Arabic and English editions. The present Masrah Ensemble-commissioned translations were developed in close collaboration between translators, guest playwrights working in English, and the authors themselves.

ACKNOWLEDGMENTS FOR THE ENGLISH EDITION

Thank you Eyad, for your animating vision, as well as for your ongoing support, counsel, and friendship.

Thank you Yasser Abu Shaqra, Eid Aziz, Sara Fakhry, Faisal Hamadah, and Nejma Zeghidi, members of our jury.

Thank you Hanan Kassab Hassan.

Thank you Milia Ayache, Zeina Halabi, Kristen Kosmas, Melanie Magidow, Dima Nasser, Antje Oegel.

Thank you Jess Barbagallo and Sam Kimball for your essential contributions to the development of the English text of Sami Nasr's *Uprooting.*

Thank you to Masrah Ensemble's many individual donors, and to Cara Levine and Hannah Rubin at Outlook Is ___ Projects for hosting a party for us. Thank you especially to Benjamin Blake, Toni Dorfman & John Gaddis, Liesel Euler, David Herskovits, John M. Sanger, and Paul Spera & Francesca Toich for generous contributions that made these translations possible.

Thank you Kate Kremer, the animating light behind 53rd State Press, for your vision, integrity, persistence, and care. Thank you to Anne DeMelo and Jess Barbagallo for your keen eyes on this manuscript.

Thank you, readers. Thank you, artists.

Thank you, Paul Spera, for your partnership in the ongoing experiment of Masrah Ensemble. Thank you, Yasser Abu Shaqra, my collaborator, for your integrity and vision.

– AB, 13 October 2025